German Fest and Traditions

Activities and Teaching Ideas for Primary Schools

Nicolette Hannam and Michelle Williams

Brilliant
PUBLICATIONS

Dedication
In memory of my lovely mum, Pauline Cranfield.
Michelle Williams.

We hope you and your pupils enjoy learning about the festivals and traditions in this book. Brilliant Publications publishes many other books for teaching modern foreign languages. To find out more details on any of the titles listed below, please log onto our website: www.brilliantpublications.co.uk.

Published by Brilliant Publications
Unit 10
Sparrow Hall Farm
Edlesborough
Dunstable
Bedfordshire
LU6 2ES, UK

Sales and stock enquiries:
Tel: 01202 712910
Fax: 0845 1309300
E-mail: brilliant@bebc.co.uk
Website: www.brilliantpublications.co.uk

General information enquiries:
Tel: 01525 222292

The name Brilliant Publications and the logo are registered trademarks.

Written by Nicolette Hannam and Michelle Williams
Illustrated by David Benham
Front cover designed by Brilliant Publications

© Text Nicolette Hannam and Michelle Williams 2009
© Design Brilliant Publications 2009

The publishers and authors would like to thank Michaela Greck-Ismair for her very careful reading of the manuscript and useful comments.

ISBN 978-1-905780-52-5

First printed and published in the UK in 2009

The right of Nicolette Hannam and Michelle Williams to be identified as the authors of this work has been asserted by themselves in accordance with the Copyright, Designs and Patents Act 1988.

Contents

Introduction

This book was written by a secondary and a primary school teacher to provide information about festivals and traditions in Germany.

Every month has ideas that support the intercultural strand of the *Framework for Modern Foreign Languages*. According to the *Framework* by the end of Year 6, most children should be able to:

◆ Demonstrate an understanding of and respect for cultural diversity
◆ Present information about an aspect of another country.

The ideas in this book can be used to develop discussions about comparisons. The *Framework* suggests comparing attitudes towards aspects of everyday life (IU6.1) and understanding differences between people (IU6.2).

It then suggests children present information about an aspect of culture through a wide variety of media. By regularly using ideas from this book you are providing your pupils with a wealth of ideas.

Each month has a choice of guided sheets that can be photocopied. There is also a wealth of suggested teaching activities, with vocabulary provided. Extension ideas are provided for more able pupils.

Running a German Day (see Planning a German Day for your School, pages 89–99) will complement your intercultural teaching and provide children with many opportunities to achieve a high standard in this area of German. The German vocabulary provided will support and reinforce your language work alongside this.

There are two analysis grids that show how and where the book covers the intercultural strand. The first (page 5) is split into year groups and shows where you can find work to cover the objectives for your own year group. The second grid (page 6) looks at each strand and shows where it is covered in the book. This will be extremely useful for MFL co-ordinators.

German Festivals and Traditions
© *Nicolette Hannam, Michelle Williams and Brilliant Publications*

Analysis by year group

Year group	Objective	Covered in book
3	Identify other languages they'd like to learn	Planning a holiday (pages 56–58)
	Learn where German is spoken	Planning a holiday (pages 56–58)
	Know some facts about one country	Throughout book
	Make contact with native speakers	Access contact through your Local Authority or the NACELL or CILT websites
	Compare different cultures	Throughout book: Viel Glück zum Gerburtstag (pages 48–50) A typical school day in Germany (pages 61–63) Comparing pastimes and everyday life (pages 64–65)
	German song/rhyme	Weihnachten (pages 81–88)
4	Know about German celebrations	Throughout book
	Identify similarities and differences in how festivals and special days are celebrated	Karneval (pages 15–18) Valentinstag (pages 19–21) Viel Glück zum Gerburtstag (pages 48–50) Weihnachten (pages 81–88)
	Use simple phrases to celebrate	Throughout book
	Compare everyday pastimes to their own	Comparing pastimes and everyday life (pages 64–65)
	Compare traditional stories	Die Märchen (pages 24–28)
5	Compare particular aspects of everyday life to their own	A typical school day in Germany (pages 61–63) Comparing pastimes and everyday life (pages 64–65)
	Exchange information with a partner school	Access contact through your Local Authority or the NACELL or CILT websites
	Compare buildings and places in contrasting localities	Comparing buildings and places (pages 74–75)
	Investigate ways of travelling to another country/countries	Planning a holiday (pages 56-58)
	Consider how cultures of different countries are incorporated into everyday life	A typical school day in Germany (pages 61–63) Comparing pastimes and everyday life (pages 64–66) How is German culture incorporated into our everyday life? (pages 69–60)
	Compare symbols and products	German symbols (pages 53–55)
6	Understand and respect cultural diversity (different attitudes)	How is German culture incorporated into our everyday life? (pages 59–60) – develop discussion from guided sheet (page 60)
	Recognize and challenge stereotypes	Challenging stereotypes (pages 78–79)
	Present information about an aspect of another country: – perform songs/plays/dramas – use ICT to present information – greater sense of audience	Year 6 pupils can choose one idea/topic from the book and use it to develop a PowerPoint presentation aimed at a given audience. Choose a specific festival from the book, eg Christmas or Easter, or they could do a geography presentation.

Analysis by objective

Learning objective		Covered in book
IU3.1	Learn about the different languages spoken by children in the school	Planning a holiday (pages 56–58). Could be developed from discussions around the German language. Does anyone speak German in our school? Which other languages are spoken? Why?
IU3.2	Locate country/countries where the language is spoken	Planning a holiday (pages 56–58)
IU3.3	Identify social conventions at home and in other cultures	Viel Glück zum Gerburtstag (pages 48–50) – typical names Social conventions addressed throughout book
IU3.4	Make direct or indirect contact with the country/countries where the language is spoken	We recommend that you approach your Local Authority for advice, or visit the NACELL or CILT websites
IU4.1	Learn about festivals and celebrations in different cultures	Throughout book
IU4.2	Know about some aspects of everyday life and compare them to their own	Throughout book, especially A typical school day in Germany (pages 61–63) and Comparing pastimes and everyday life (pages 64–65)
IU4.3	Compare traditional stories	Die Märchen (pages 24–28)
IU4.4	Learn about ways of travelling to the country/countries	Planning a holiday (pages 56–58)
IU5.1	Look at further aspects of their everyday lives from the perspective of someone from another country	Guided sheet – What I know about Germany (page 76) See also, German Day evaluation sheet (pages 98–99)
IU5.2	Recognize similarities and differences between places	Throughout book Planning a holiday (pages 56–58) – comparing two localities Comparing buildings and places (pages 74–76)
IU5.3	Compare symbols, objects or products which represent their own culture with those of another country	German symbols (pages 53–55) Das Essen (pages 29–34) Planning a holiday (pages 56–58) – develop from locality discussion
IU6.1	Compare attitudes towards aspects of everyday life	A typical school day in Germany (pages 61–63) Comparing pastimes and everyday life (pages 64–65) Role models for children (page 80) Das Essen (pages 29–34)
IU6.2	Recognize and understand some of the differences between people	Throughout book – comparing how people celebrate How is German culture incorporated into our everyday lives? (pages 59–60) – develop cultural diversity discussion from guided sheet (page 60) Challenging stereotypes (pages 78–79)
IU6.3	Present information about an aspect of culture	Children can be encouraged to develop plays, songs and dances from the information taught about German culture They can use ICT (for example, PowerPoint) to present information for a given audience Can possibly be used for transition information/ assessment

Successful teaching Ideas for new vocabulary

There are many ways to help children learn new vocabulary and it is important to use a variety of methods and make it fun. Below are some successful ideas that have been tried and tested:

◆ Very simply, hold up flashcards and ask the children to repeat the words after you. They like doing this in different voices.

◆ Mime a card. Children have to guess the word, in German.

◆ Which flashcard am I holding? Hold flashcard facing you. Ask children to guess which one you are looking at. This tests memory and pronunciation.

◆ True or False. Children only repeat the flashcard after you if you are saying the word that matches it.

◆ Matching cards. Give out cards to match yours, for example with names of pets. Say a word and children hold up the matching card, if they have it.

◆ Children could sequence the words as you call them out.

◆ Children could stand in order with flashcards, for example with names of the months. Or they could stand in alphabetical order.

◆ For colours, they could build towers in the order that you call out, using coloured bricks.

◆ Children could hold up key words as they hear them in a song.

◆ Children could draw what you say, using mini-whiteboards.

◆ Slap the flashcard! Or the correct part of a picture (for example, the face). Children come up to the board in pairs (boys versus girls is popular). They use their hands to touch (slap) the flashcard the teacher says. A point is given to the first one to touch the correct flashcard.

◆ Teach the children actions to go with the songs you learn.

◆ Use puppets or soft toys to ask and answer questions.

◆ Give the children cards with words and pictures and use them to play Pelmanism (also known as Pairs).

◆ As above, but play Snap.

◆ Picture lotto. Cross off pictures as you hear the word called out.

◆ Pictionary. The teacher can draw pictures, for example pets, and children call out as soon as they recognize it. Or they can play in small groups, on mini-whiteboards.

◆ *Galgenspiel* (Hangman).

◆ *Simon sagt* (Simon says).

◆ Chinese Whispers.

◆ Kim's Game.

Neujahrstag

New Year's Day

Background information

New Year's Eve is called Silvester in Germany, after Pope Silvester I, who died on 31st December 335. Germans love fireworks and at the stroke of midnight the sky is lit up with fireworks. Berlin hosts one of the biggest New Year's Eve celebrations in Europe, with fireworks around the Brandenburg Gate.

German people usually spend New Year's Day celebrating with their family wishing each other, 'Ein schönes neues Jahr!' or Happy New Year. Traditionally families meet to eat lunch together. It is traditional to eat carp or herring (types of fish) with toast and to drink champagne. Cabbage is eaten to bring financial stability and people share meat or cheese fondue with family and friends. Children are often given extra pocket money.

People give each other little symbols of luck made out of marzipan or chocolate. Little pigs *(Glücksschwein)* are popular, as are four leaf clovers, ladybirds or chimney sweeps.

Just as in many countries, people in Germany make New Year's resolutions. Some people choose to give New Year's cards rather than Christmas cards. They may write inside how their family have spent the last year.

German Festivals and Traditions
© *Nicolette Hannam, Michelle Williams and Brilliant Publications*

Teaching activities

◆ Use the photocopiable sheet on page 10 to describe your New Year celebrations to an imaginary or real German friend.

◆ Discuss and compare how New Year's Day is celebrated in Germany and in Britain.

◆ Design a New Year's Day card. Include details of what will be studied throughout the year in German lessons to inform parents.

◆ Design a New Year's Day menu (*Neujahrs Speisekarte*) in German, using the German foods you know.

◆ Draw and label some key foods eaten in Germany on New Year's Day. (See Schlüsselwörter for vocabulary.)

◆ Draw a special meal that you have eaten recently and label it in German. Use a dictionary as support.

◆ Discuss your New Year's resolutions in a group. What are they? Are they achievable? How?

◆ Can you set any New Year's resolutions for your class or your school?

◆ Draw and describe your ideal New Year's Day. Who would you spend it with? Where? What would you do? What would you eat?

◆ Use the Internet to research different festivals and traditions for New Year's Day in Germany and other countries.

◆ Write a list of five questions that you would all like to research about life in Germany.

Schlüsselwörter

Ein schönes neues Jahr	Happy New Year
Ein Vorsatz für das neues Jahr	New Year Resolution
das Feuerwerk	fireworks
der Karpfen	carp
der Hering	herring
der Toast	toast
der Sekt	sparkling wine
der Kohl	cabbage
die Karotten	carrots
das Fleisch	meat
der Käse	cheese
das Glücksschwein	lucky pig
Neujahrs Speisekarte	A New Year's Day menu
die Vorspeise	starter
die Hauptspeise	main course
der Nachtisch	dessert
die Getränke	drinks

Neujahrstag

Name: Datum:

I can describe how I celebrate New Year.

Use the space below to write a letter to an imaginary German pen friend. Introduce yourself and explain where you live. Describe how you celebrate New Year. What do you eat? What do you do? Who do you spend it with? Can you explain the reasons for any of your traditions?

Extension activity

Write some questions that you could ask a German friend about New Year. Are there any other questions you would like to ask?

German Festivals and Traditions
© Nicolette Hannam, Michelle Williams and Brilliant Publications

Heilige Drei Könige

The Three Holy Kings

Background information

Heilige Drei Könige takes place on the 6th January. The date for the celebration of Christ's birth has fluctuated throughout history. January 6th was the day of celebration until the Roman church adopted December 25th in the fourth century. Today the 6th January is known as Epiphany or *Heilige Drei Könige* (The Three Holy Kings) in Germany. In many parts of Europe, including Austria, Germany and Switzerland, Christmas celebrations do not end until the date. January 6th is considered to be the date of the arrival of the Three Kings in Bethlehem and the end of the 'twelve days of Christmas'. In German the Three Kings or the 'Magi' are called König Balthasar, König Melchior, and König Caspar.

Children dress up as the Three Kings and go from house to house holding up a large paper star. They wish people a 'Happy New Year', sing carols and often collect money for charity. They are called *Sternsinger*, which literally means 'star singer'. Traditionally the initials C + M + B and the year are written in chalk on the front door. For example C + M + B 09, which in Latin means *Christus mansionem benedicat* (Christ bless this house). It is believed that this brings good luck for the year ahead. C + M + B also signify the initials of the names of the Three Kings: Caspar, Melchior and Balthasar. The child who plays Melchior usually colours his/her face black, because one of the kings was said to be of black ethnic origin.

A special dessert called *Dreikönigskuchen* or Three Kings Cake can be served on the evening of 6th January. This is a sweet cake made with dried fruits topped with a sugared glaze.

In some Catholic countries, Twelfth Night or Epiphany, marks the start of the Carnival season.

Teaching activities

◆ Explain to the children about the tradition of the *Heilige Drei Könige*.

◆ Investigate the Three Kings Cake on the Internet.

◆ Mime making the *Dreikönigskuchen* as you describe the actions in German (see recipe on page 13).

◆ Make the cake using the recipe.

◆ Children could design and make a recipe card for the *Dreikönigskuchen*.

◆ Draw and name the three kings. What do you know about them? What else could we find out?

◆ Design some new outfits for the three kings.

◆ Link to PSCHE and talk about charity. What is it? Who is it? Why does it exist? What can we do to help?

◆ Children could 'role play' visiting their friends to wish them Happy New Year, 'Ein schönes neues Jahr.' They could use other greetings they know, such as 'Guten Tag!' (Hello), 'Hallo' (Hi) or Auf Wiedersehen/Tschüs! (See you soon/Bye).

◆ Children could use the guided sheet on page 14 to record their knowledge of *Drei Heilige Könige*.

Schlüsselwörter

Heilige Drei Könige	Three Holy Kings
Sternsinger	Star singer
der Goldstern	gold star
Ein schönes neues Jahr	Happy New Year
Guten Tag	Hello
Hallo	Hi
Auf Wiedersehen	See you soon
Tschüs	Bye
die Butter	butter
der Zucker	sugar
das Mehl	flour
die Milch	milk
das Ei	egg
die Mandel	almond

German Festivals and Traditions
© Nicolette Hannam, Michelle Williams and Brilliant Publications

Dreikönigskuchen

Ingredients

500g flour
1 tsp salt
75g sugar
8g dried yeast
75g melted butter or margarine
approx. 3 dessertspoons (30ml) of milk
1 beaten egg
approx. 100g flaked almonds for decoration
zest of 1 lemon
50g candied peel
1 whole almond or apeice of chocolate for
    the king
a crown

Instructions

◆ Warm the milk slightly and stir in the sugar
    and yeast.

◆ Put half the egg to one side and kneed
    together the remaining ingredients.

◆ Cover and leave for approximately 1 hour,
    until the mixture has doubled.

◆ Make 9 balls. Form 8 x 60g balls and use
    the rest for the centre piece. Hide the
    almond or chocolate in one of the balls.

◆ Place the big ball of dough in the middle of
    a baking tray. Place the 8 small dough balls
    around it in a circle.

◆ Glaze the cake with the remaining egg and
    sprinkle with the flaked almonds.

◆ Bake for around 30 mins at 180°C. Take
    out and leave to cool. Serve with the crown
    on top.

Zutaten

500g Mehl
1 Teelöffel Salz
75g Zucker
8g Trockenhefe
75g Butter oder Margarine, weich
ca. 30ml Milch
1 Ei, verklopft
ca 100g Mandelblättchen zum Bestreuen
1 Zitronenschale
50g Orangeat
1 Mandel oder 1 Stück Schokolade für den
    König
eine Krone

Zubereitung

◆ Die Milch etwas erwärmen, den Zucker
    und die Hefe dazu rühren.

◆ Danach alle Zutaten aber nur das halbe Ei
    zusammen kneten.

◆ Zugedeckt bei Raumtemperatur ca. 1 Std.
    ums Doppelte aufgehen lassen.

◆ Aus einem Teil des Teiges 8 Portionen zu
    je ca. 60g abwägen, restlichen Teig für die
    Mitte verwenden. 9 Kugeln formen, dabei
    die ganze Mandel als König in eine der
    Kugeln stecken.

◆ Platziere die grosse Kugel in der Mitte
    des Backbleches und verteile die kleinen
    darum herum.

◆ Den Kuchen vor dem Backen mit dem
    beiseite gestellten Ei bestreichen, und mit
    den Mandelblättchen bestreuen.

◆ Etwa 30 Min. in der unteren Hälfte des
    auf 180 Grad vorgeheizten Ofens backen.
    Herausnehmen, auskühlen lassen.

Heilige Drei Könige

Name: Datum:

I understand how *Heilige Drei Könige* is celebrated in Germany.

Imagine it is the day of *Heilige Drei Könige*. You are celebrating with your family and friends.

Design and draw a picture of your outfit. Don't forget to carry your *Goldstern* (gold star).

Which family and friends would you invite? Write in a sentence, using commas.

Extension activity

◆ Use the Internet to find out about Epiphany in Germany and in different countries.

German Festivals and Traditions
© Nicolette Hannam, Michelle Williams and Brilliant Publications

Karneval
Carnival time

Background information

Karneval is prevalent in many countries and signals the beginning of Lent. The word comes from the Latin for 'take off the flesh' and it is a time when people would make the most of eating fatty foods before fasting for Lent began.

The *Karneval* season officially begins at 11.11am on the 11th November (11th day of the 11th month). However, it is suspended for Advent and Christmas and most of the celebrations take place in the week leading up to Ash Wednesday (*Aschermittwoch*). During that week parades take place from Saturday to Tuesday, the most important ones being on *Rosenmontag* (Rose Monday). The Karneval season is often referred to as *die fünfte Jahreszeit* (the fifth season).

Karneval is not a national holiday in Germany, but in many areas schools are closed on *Rosenmontag* and the following Tuesday.

The way *Karneval* is celebrated varies enormously from region to region, and is particularly strong in the Catholic south and west of Germany. Even the name of the festivals varies. It is known as *Karneval* in Rhineland, *Fassenacht* in Mainz, *Fasching* in Bavaria and *Fastnacht* in southwest Germany. Across Germany the celebrations are organized by local carnival clubs, which every year choose ein Prinz (a prince) and sometimes also eine Prinzessin (a princess). Every town boasts at least one parade with floats and usually *Kamelle* (sweets) are thrown into the crowds.

In addition to parades there are lots of masked balls, sometimes on specific themes. The balls are held in big public halls. The carnival prince comes to these events for a dance, often accompanied by his *Hofstaat* (royal household), jokers and *Funkenmariechen*. The *Funkenmariechen* are dance groups of young women and girls, in special uniforms with very short skirts. They do acrobatic dancing (similar in style to cheerleading). There are also lots of *Hausbälle* (house balls) in private houses. People invite friends and relatives for a masked ball at their house. Other typical events are street parties, processions and fireworks.

The traditional carnival greeting varies from region to region. 'Hellau!' is the most common, however, there are many variations. For example, in Köln the traditional greeting is 'Alaaf!', in southern Germany people call out 'Narri Narro!' and in Mannheim they shout 'Ahoi!'.

Some of Germany's best-known celebrations are held in Cologne (Köln) and Mainz.

Cologne Carnival

The Cologne Carnival, with its street parties and parades, is organized by a Festival Committee, whose job it is to coordinate and regulate the activities of well over 100 carnival associations. The Committee was founded in 1823.

Every year, three people pay for the privilege of dressing up as the *Jungfrau* (virgin), *Prinz* (prince) and the *Bauer* (farmer or peasant). This custom has its origins in the Middle Ages, when the carnival celebrations allowed people to temporarily overturn the tightly structured class system, with peasants disguised as princes, mixing with aristocrats disguised as farmers. The carnival prince is seen as the most important and leads most of the parades. And strangely enough, the *Jungfrau* is usually male!

Celebrations begin with *Weiberfastnacht* (Carnival of Women) on the Thursday before Ash Wednesday. Women line the streets in fancy dress, heading for the town centre or town hall. Women assume total power on this day.

Over a million people attend the carnival, particularly on *Rosenmontag*. In addition to *Kamelle* (sweets), little bottles of *Kölnischwasser* (eau de Cologne) are thrown into the crowd during the processions! There are also several events which run alongside the processions in local bars and clubs.

German Festivals and Traditions
© Nicolette Hannam, Michelle Williams and Brilliant Publications

Teaching activities

◆ Design a *Karneval* float for a procession. Use the vocabulary to help you.

◆ Design your *Karneval* costume or a *Karnevalmaske* (carnival mask).

◆ Use the Internet to compare the Cologne Carnival to The Notting Hill Festival.

◆ Plan a Carnival Day for your school. What could people wear? What could they eat? How would you explain the religious reasons behind a carnival?

◆ Design a poster advertising the Cologne Carnival.

◆ Write an acrostic poem with the heading 'Carnival'.

◆ Write a diary entry of an exciting trip to a carnival.

◆ Design *ein Kostüm* (a costume) for *der Prinz* and *die Prinzessin*.

◆ Make an invitation to a *Karneval* party. Use the template below or design your own.

Schlüsselwörter

Aschermittwoch	Ash Wednesday
Die Fastenzeit	Lent
Faschingsdienstag	
	Shrove Tuesday
Rosenmontag	Rose Monday
die Fünfte Jahreszeit	fifth season
der Prinz	prince
die Prinzessin	princess
ein Kostümfest	masked ball
eine Maske	a mask
ein Festwagen	a float
ein Kostüm	a costume
eine Parade	a parade
die Funkenmariechen	
	dancing girls
die Hausbälle	house ball
der Hofstaat	royal household
die Jungfrau	virgin
der Bauer	farmer or peasant
die Weiberfastnacht	
	Carnival of Women
die Kamelle	sweets
das Kölnischwasser	
	eau de Cologne

Partyeinladung
Kommt zu meiner Party

Datum:

Uhr:

Addresse:

◆ Children can use the guided sheet on page 18 to imagine and record a *Karneval* celebration.

◆ Use the Internet to find out how *Karneval* is celebrated in different countries.

Karneval

Name: Datum:

I understand how and why *Karneval* is celebrated in Germany.

Imagine you are in a town in Germany, celebrating *Karneval* with your friends and family.

What can you see?

What can you hear?

Extension activities

◆ Can you design a Karneval costume? Label the costume in German, using a dictionary.

◆ Use the Internet to find out how Karneval is celebrated in different countries.

German Festivals and Traditions

Valentinstag
Valentine's Day

Background information

Germany has only recently started to celebrate St Valentine's Day. As in this country, it is celebrated on 14th February, when people send romantic cards and presents to each other.

Here is a traditional German Valentine's Day Poem:

Rosen, Tulpen, Nelken	Roses, tulips and carnations
Alle Blumen welken	All flowers wilt
Nur die eine welkt nicht	The only one that doesn't
Und die heißt Vergissmeinnicht.	Is called a 'Forget me not'.

Teaching activities

◆ Make a Valentine's Day card or poster. Write some words on the board to help:

Einen schönen Valentinstag	Happy Valentine's Day
Lieber …	Dear … (boy)
Liebe ...	Dear … (girl)
Mit Liebe von	Love from

◆ Make a 'Chatterbox' finger game (see page 20 for instructions).

Here are some suggestions for things that could be written inside:

Ich liebe dich	I love/like you
Ich liebe dich nicht	I don't love/like you
Du bist wunderbar	You're great
Willst du mit mir ausgehen?	Will you go out with me?
Willst du mich heiraten?	Will you marry me?
Wie heißt du?	What is your name?

> **Schlüsselwörter**
>
> | | |
> |---|---|
> | die Liebe | love |
> | die Freundschaft | friendship |
> | Ich liebe dich | I love/like you |
> | Ich liebe dich nicht | I don't love/like you |
> | Willst du mich heiraten? | Will you marry me? |
> | Einen schönen Valentinstag | Happy Valentine's Day |
> | lieber … | dear … (boy) |
> | liebe ... | dear … (girl) |
> | Mit Liebe von | love from |
> | du bist wunderbar | you're great |
> | Willst du mit mir ausgehen? | Will you go out with me? |
> | Wie heißt du? | What's your name? |

Pupils could use any German vocabulary they have learned for the words on the outside flaps, eg colours, numbers etc.

◆ Children could use the guided sheet on page 21 to design a Valentine's Day card or poster using German vocabulary.

◆ You could try some freeze framing. Ask some children to freeze in a traditional Valentine's Day pose (for example, man on one knee, proposing) then, as a class, discuss what each character is thinking, feeling and saying.

Chatterbox

How to make a chatterbox

1   Fold a square piece of paper in half vertically and horizontally, and then unfold.

2   Fold all four corners so they meet at the centre point. Turn the folded square over.

3   Fold all four new corners so they meet at the centre point.

4   Fold the top edge to meet the bottom edge, crease the fold and unfold again. Fold the right edge to meet the left one, crease and unfold.

5   Hold the chatterbox as shown. Slip the pointer finger and thumb from each hand under the square flaps at the back, pinching the folds.

6. Practise opening and closing the 'mouth' of the chatterbox.

7   Write a word on each of the four corners. Open the chatterbox up and write other words on all eight triangles, or put coloured dots. Finally, lift up the flaps and write your chosen sentences underneath each triangle. You are now ready to play!

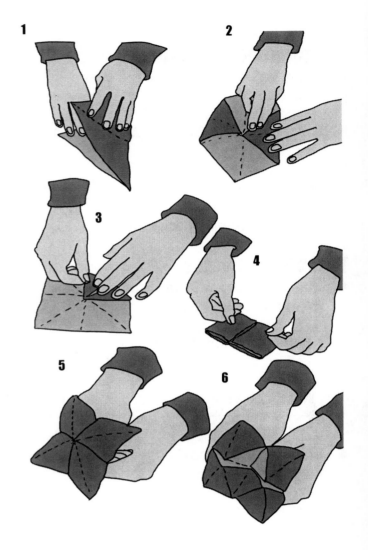

How to use a chatterbox

◆   Ask your friend to read each of the words displayed on the outside of the chatterbox and to choose one word. Spell out the word, using the German alphabet, opening and closing the chatterbox as you say each letter.

◆   At the end of spelling this word, four of the inside words, or coloured dots, will be displayed. Ask your friend to read, or name, them and to choose one.

◆   Spell out that chosen word, opening and closing the 'bird's beak' again as you say each letter. At the end of this spelling, four of the inside words will be displayed. It may be the same four words or it may be the other four words.

◆   Ask your friend to read these four words and to choose one again. Open up the chosen flap.

◆   Read out the sentence under the flap and see how your partner responds!

German Festivals and Traditions
© Nicolette Hannam, Michelle Williams and Brilliant Publications

Valentinstag

Name: Datum:

I learned about *Valentinstag* in Germany

Design a Valentine's Day card or poster. Use some of the German words we have learned.

Play with your 'Chatterbox' with your friends. In this box write down the German words that you chose to use.

Extension activities

◆ Can you compare and contrast how you celebrate 'Valentine's Day?'

◆ Write a letter to an imaginary or real German person to tell them how you celebrate.

Die Berlinale
The Berlin International Film Festival

Background information

The Berlin International Film Festival is one of the world's leading film festivals. Founded in 1951, the festival has been celebrated annually in February since 1978. It was established by the Americans after World War II in an attempt to return Berlin to how it was before the war. Alfred Hitchcock's film 'Rebecca' opened the first festival. The awards are called the Golden and Silver Bears.

The Festival is Berlin's largest cultural event and also one of the most important dates on the international film industry's calendar. It is a massive event with more than 200,000 tickets sold and up to 400 films shown each year. Films are shown in glamorous cinemas across the city. For two weeks, art, glamour, parties and business take place at the *Berlinale*. It has become a good rival for the Cannes Film Festival.

Teaching activities

◆ Find out as much information as you can about the *Berlinale*. Use the Internet to help you.

◆ What would you wear to this famous festival? Design an outfit using the photocopiable sheet on page 23.

◆ Make a poster advertising your favourite film. Can you explain why you would choose it to win awards?

◆ Design a glamorous cinema that has been commissioned to be built for the next Berlin Film Festival.

◆ Design posters and tickets for the Festival.

◆ You could incorporate some maths work based on the Euro.

◆ Write a newspaper report of the latest festival. Who won? Why? Make up a quotation from them. What did they wear? Describe their film.

◆ Record or act out a short television broadcast showing live from the event.

◆ Compare statistics from the Cannes Film Festival and the Berlin Film Festival. Which one would you choose to go to? Why?

Schlüsselwörter

ein Film	a film
ein Schauspieler	an actor
eine Schauspielerin	an actress
ein Regisseur	a director
ein Produtent	a producer
ein roter Teppich	a red carpet
ein Musiker	a musician
eine gefeierte Persönlichkeit/	a famous person/
ein Star	a celebrity
Es war wunderbar!	It was amazing!
Es hat mir gefallen!	I loved it!
Fünf Sterne!	Five stars!

Die Berlinale

Name: Datum:

I had fun learning about the Berlin Film Festival.

Imagine you are a famous actor or actress, you are just about to go down the red carpet! Draw a picture of the scene.

Describe in writing what you would see and hear!

Extension activity

Can you find out some more information about Berlin? Use the Internet and/or information books and write six key points about this city.

Die Märchen
Fairy tales

Background information

Jakob Ludwig Grimm and Wilhelm Karl Grimm were born in Hannau, Germany, on January 4, 1785, and February 24, 1786, respectively. As the brothers grew up they became fascinated by the folk poetry and tales they heard and when they got older they decided to write them down. So the collection of Grimm's Fairy tales began, the first volume was published in 1812 and was called *Kinder-und Hausmärchen* or 'Children and Household Tales'. In all they collected over 200 stories. They are particularly famous for Rumplestiltskin, Snow White, Sleeping Beauty, Rapunzel, Cinderella and Hansel and Gretel.

Wilhelm and Jacob Grimm also had many other books and journals published, on German folklore and linguistics.

Here are the titles of some fairy tales in German:

Rotkäppchen	Little Red Riding Hood
Dornröschen	Sleeping Beauty
Schneewittchen und die Sieben Zwerge	Snow White and the Seven Dwarfs
Rapunzel	Rapunzel
Rumpelstilzchen	Rumplestiltskin
Aschenputtel	Cinderella
Hänsel und Gretel	Hansel and Gretel

Teaching activities

◆ Read a simple fairy tale for the children to act out. Familiarize them with the key vocabulary first. Display the fairy tale for the children to follow as you read it aloud.

◆ Ask the children to respond with physical gestures when they hear key words or character's names. Use lots of repetition.

◆ Use a simple German fairy tale in a sequencing activity. Jumble up key sentences for the children to reorder.

◆ Ask the children to pretend to be a character, for example Red Riding Hood. What could we ask her? Children could ask them their name / age / favourite colour, and so on.

◆ Can the children use simple German to change the beginning or the ending of the story? They could be given a choice of two endings, in German, that they have to translate and choose.

Schlüsselwörter

Es war einmal …	Once upon a time …
der König	the king
die Königin	the queen
die Prinzessin	the princess
der Prinz	the prince
die Fee	the fairy
die gute Fee	fairy godmother
der Forst	the forest
der Wald	the wood
das Schloss	the palace
der Wolf	the wolf
die Großmutter	grandma
die Sieben Zwergen	the seven dwarfs
der Zauberstab	a magic wand
das Biest	the beast
das Ungeheuer	the monster
ein Holzhacker	the woodcutter
der Palast	the castle
die Hexe	the wicked witch
die Stiefschwestern	the step sisters
ein Kürbis	a pumpkin
der goldene Schuh	the gold slipper
die Maus	the mouse
Spiegelein, Spiegelein an der Wand, wer ist die Schönste im ganzen Land?	Mirror, mirror on the wall who is the fairest of them all?

◆ Which stories do you think these rhymes come from?

Spiegelein, Spiegelein an der Wand
Wer ist die Schönste im ganzen Land?

Mirror, mirror on the wall
Who's the fairest of them all?

Großmutter, was hast du für große Ohren!
Damit ich dich besser hören kann!

Grandmother, what big ears you have!
All the better to hear you with.

◆ Copy out the German rhymes and illustrate them.

◆ Children could match German characters names and key words to German fairy tale titles. Suggested answers are in the chart below:

Rotkäppchen *(Little Red Riding Hood)*	**Dornröschen** *(Sleeping Beauty)*	**Aschenputtel** *(Cinderella)*	**Rapunzel** *(Rapunzel)*
Rotkäppchen (Little Red Riding Hood) Es war einmal ein kleines Mädchen … (Once upon a time there was a little girl …) Der Wald (the wood) Der Wolf (the wolf) Die Großmutter (the Grandmother) Die Oma (Granny) Ein Holzhacker (a woodcutter)	Dornröschen (Sleeping Beauty) Es war einmal … (Once upon a time …) Ein König (a king) Eine Königin (a queen) Ein Königssohn (a king's son) Das Schloss (the castle) Eine Spindel (a spindle) Ein hundertjähriger tiefer Schlaf (a 100 year sleep) Er gab ihm einen Kuss (He kissed her)	Aschenputtel (Cinderella) Die Stiefschwestern (the stepsisters) Die Stiefmutter (the stepmother) Der Prinz (Prince) Das Fest (the Party) Der goldene Schuh (the gold slipper)	Es war einmal … (Once upon a time …) Eine Zauberin (a witch) Der Wald (the wood) Ein Turm (the tower) Ein Königssohn (the King's son) Rapunzel,Rapunzel laß mir dein Haar herunter (Rapunzel,Rapunzel Let down your hair)

◆ Use the Red Riding Hood dialogue on page 27. Children could act it out in assembly. Or each phrase could be given to the children to match to a character. A translation is given below):

(Rotkäppchen meets the wolf in the forest.)		
Rotkäppchen:	Hallo. Ich heiße Rotkäppchen.	Hello. My name is Little Red Riding Hood.
Der Wolf:	Guten Tag Rotkäppchen, wohin gehst du?	Hello Little Red Riding Hood, where are you going?
Rotkäppchen:	Ich besuche meine Oma.	I'm visiting my granny.

(The wolf goes to Grandma's house, dressed as Rotkäppchen.)

Der Wolf:	Hallo Großmutter.	Hello, Granny.
Oma:	Hallo Rotkäppchen, wie geht's?	Hello, Little Red Riding Hood. How are you?
Der Wolf:	Mir geht's gut, danke und dir?	I'm well, how are you?
Oma:	Nicht so gut. Komm herein.	Not so well. Come in.

(The wolf eats Grandma and disguises himself as her).

Rotkäppchen:	Hallo Großmutter!	Hello Grandma!
Der Wolf:	Hallo mein Liebling, komm herein.	Hello darling, come in.
Rotkäppchen:	Oma, was hast du für große Augen!	Granny, what big eyes you have!
Der Wolf:	Damit ich dich besser sehen kann!	All the better to see you with.
Rotkäppchen:	Oma, was hast du für große Ohren!	Granny, what big ears you have!
Der Wolf:	Damit ich dich besser hören kann!	All the better to hear you with.
Rotkäppchen:	Oma, was hast du für große Zähne!	Granny, what big teeth you have!
Der Wolf:	Damit ich dich besser FRESSEN kann!	All the better to eat you with!
Rotkäppchen:	Hilfe!	Help!

(The woodcutter runs in the house and saves Rotkäppchen – and cuts open wolf's stomach to save Grandma.)

Rotkäppchen und Oma:	Vielen Dank!	Thank you very much, Sir.
Ende		*The end*

◆ Children could use the guided sheet on page 28 to make up their own picture story of a fairy tale.

Rotkäppchen

(Rotkäppchen meets the wolf in the forest.)

Rotkäppchen:	Hallo. Ich heiße Rotkäppchen.
Der Wolf:	Guten Tag Rotkäppchen, wohin gehst du?
Rotkäppchen:	Ich besuche meine Oma.

(The wolf goes to Grandma's house, dressed as Rotkäppchen.)

Der Wolf:	Hallo Großmutter.
Oma:	Hallo Rotkäppchen, wie geht's?
Der Wolf:	Mir geht's gut, danke und dir?
Oma:	Nicht so gut. Komm herein.

(The wolf eats Grandma and disguises himself as her).

Rotkäppchen:	Hallo Großmutter!
Der Wolf:	Hallo mein Liebling, komm herein.
Rotkäppchen:	Oma, was hast du für große Augen!
Der Wolf:	Damit ich dich besser sehen kann!
Rotkäppchen:	Oma, was hast du für große Ohren!
Der Wolf:	Damit ich dich besser hören kann!
Rotkäppchen:	Oma, was hast du für große Zähne!
Der Wolf:	Damit ich dich besser FRESSEN kann!
Rotkäppchen:	Hilfe!

(The woodcutter runs in the house and saves Rotkäppchen – and cuts open wolf's stomach to save Grandma.)

Rotkäppchen: und Oma:	Vielen Dank!

Ende

Die Märchen

Name: Datum:

I have learned about die Gebrüder Grimm and fairy tales in German.

Can you make up your own picture story of a fairy tale? Use the vocabulary you have learned.

Can you draw some of your own German fairy tale characters? Can you label their clothes (including the colours) in German?

German Festivals and Traditions
© Nicolette Hannam, Michelle Williams and Brilliant Publications

Das Essen
German food

Background information

When people think of German food, sauerkraut, sausages and beer often spring to mind! But German food has so much more to offer.

Das Frühstück

Breakfast or *das Frühstück* is considered by many as the most important meal of the day. It usually consists of bread, jam, coffee, tea or hot chocolate. Sometimes people eat a selection of cheeses, cold meats, eggs, yoghurt and fruit.

Das Mittagessen

Lunch or *das Mittagessen* is traditionally the main family meal eaten at 12–1 pm. Lunch usually consists of meat with pasta or potatoes and vegetables or a salad.

Das Abendessen

Dinner or *das Abendessen* is usually a cold meal of bread, sausages, cheese and salad.

Kaffe und Kuchen

Germany is well known for its tradition of *Kaffee und Kuchen*. People indulge in coffee and cakes between 2–4 pm. The type of cake depends on the season. During the carnival season jam doughnuts or *Berliner* are traditional. In the summer people eat *Pflaumenkuchen* or *Erdbeerkuchen* (plum or strawberry flans) with *Schlagsahne* (whipped cream). In winter (mainly at Christmas time), *Stollen* is eaten; this is a cake filled with dried fruits and marzipan. And finally, *die Schwarzwälder Kirschtorte* or Black Forest Gateau is a well-known cake, originating in South West Germany. This is a chocolate cake layered with cream and cherries and was first mentioned in writing as early as 1934.

Die Wurst

Sausages and cold meats are firm German favourites. There are about 1500 different types of sausage and each region has its own specialities. You would have to live in Germany a long time to sample all of them! Here are some of the more well-known examples:

◆ **Frankfurters**
   Strictly speaking, sausages should only be given the name 'Frankfurter' if they are made in and around Frankfurt. They are, however, made all over Germany. Frankfurters are made from top quality, lean pork mixed with salt, bacon fat and spices.

◆ **Knackwurst**

These are very similar to Frankfurters but are shorter and fatter. They get their name from the cracking sound that is made when the skin splits.

◆ **Bockwurst**

These are made from finely ground beef and pork. They are smoked until they are pink and are larger than Frankfurters.

◆ **Bratwurst**

These are much paler in colour and are fried or grilled. Bratwurst are made from pure pork or veal.

◆ **Bierwurst**

'Beer sausage' is made from pork and beef and there is no beer in the recipe at all. It gets its name because it goes well with beer!

Sausages are traditionally served with *Brötchen* (bread rolls), *Senf* (mustard) and *Sauerkraut* (pickled white cabbage). You might like yours with *Pommes* (chips)!

Bier

Germany is also famous for its beer and there are thousands of different varieties, many of which are brewed in small, local breweries.

German Festivals and Traditions
© Nicolette Hannam, Michelle Williams and Brilliant Publications

Teaching activities

- Children could learn the names of the shops that food comes from, eg *das Brot* (bread) from *die Bäckerei* (the bakery). They could draw the food that is sold in each of the shops on the photocopiable sheet on page 33.

- Compare shops in Germany to those in Britain. In both countries many people now shop in large supermarkets to save time.

- Children could role play buying items in a shop, first as a whole class and then in small groups or pairs. They could extend their learning by adding size or colour information.

- Give children names of food to put in alphabetical order.

- Role play being in a café.

- Use a dictionary to translate your school dinner (or packed lunch) today into German.

- Draw and label typical German meal using the photocopiable sheet on page 34.

- Make *Glühwein ... für Kinder* using the recipes on page 32.

- Children could mime making the *Glühwein* as you describe the actions in German (see recipe on page 32).

- Design and make a recipe card for the *Glühwein* recipe.

- Compare and contrast German and British foods.

- Write to an imaginary or real German pen pal and explain some traditional foods that you eat. Describe the foods.

- Use the Internet to find some more German foods and see if you can find a recipe!

Schlüsselwörter

das Frühstück	breakfast
das Mittagessen	lunch
das Abendessen	dinner
Kaffee und Kuchen	coffee and cakes
die Wurst	sausage
der Senf	mustard
das Sauerkraut	pickled white cabbage
Pommes	chips
das Bier	beer
die Bäckerei	the bakery
das Brot	bread
das Brötchen	bread rolls
die Konditorei	the cake shop
der Kuchen	cake
Berliner	jam doughnuts
der Pflaumenkuchen	plum flan
der Erdbeerkuchen	strawberry flan
die Schwarzwälder Kirschtorte	Black Forest Gateau
die Metzgerei	butchers
das Essen	food
der Schinken	ham
der Markt	the market
die Bananen	bananas
die Äpfel	apples
die Birnen	pears

Glühwein ... für Kinder

Served warm. Usually made with red wine.

Ingredients
4 cups of apple juice
2 cups of black tea
2 tablespoons sugar
1 lemon
1 orange
1 cinnamon stick
2 cloves

Instructions
◆ Put the apple juice and tea in a saucepan and heat slowly.

◆ Peel and juice the lemon and orange. Save the peel.

◆ Place the juice, peel, sugar and spices in the pan and continue to cook.

◆ Do not boil.

◆ Taste and adjust the spices.

◆ Strain the mixture through a sieve.

◆ Pour in a glass and serve hot.

Zutaten
4 Tassen Apfelsaft
4 Tassen Schwarztee
2 Esslöffel Zucker
1 Zitrone
1 Apfelsine
1 Zimtstauge
2 Gerwürznelken

Zubereitung
◆ Apfelsaft mit Schwarztee in einen Topf geben und langsam erwärmen

◆ Die Früchte auspressen und die Schale bei Seiten stellen.

◆ Saft, Schale, Zucker und Gewürze in den Topf geben und erwärmen.

◆ Der Glühwein darf nicht kochen.

◆ Nach Geschmack süßen.

◆ Den Glühwein durch ein Teesieb gießen.

◆ In ein Glas füllen und heiß trinken

German Festivals and Traditions
© *Nicolette Hannam, Michelle Williams and Brilliant Publications*

Das Essen

Name: Datum:

I know where you can buy food in Germany.

Der Markt

Die Bäckerei

Die Konditorei

Die Metzgerei

Now use a dictionary to look up some words for items that might be sold in *der Supermarkt* (supermarket). Carefully write the words in the supermarket trolley.

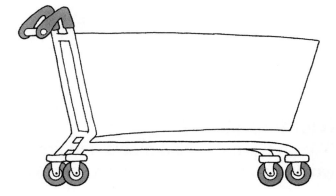

Das Essen

Name: Datum:

I have learned about some traditional German foods and drinks.

Draw and label some typical German meals on the plates below:

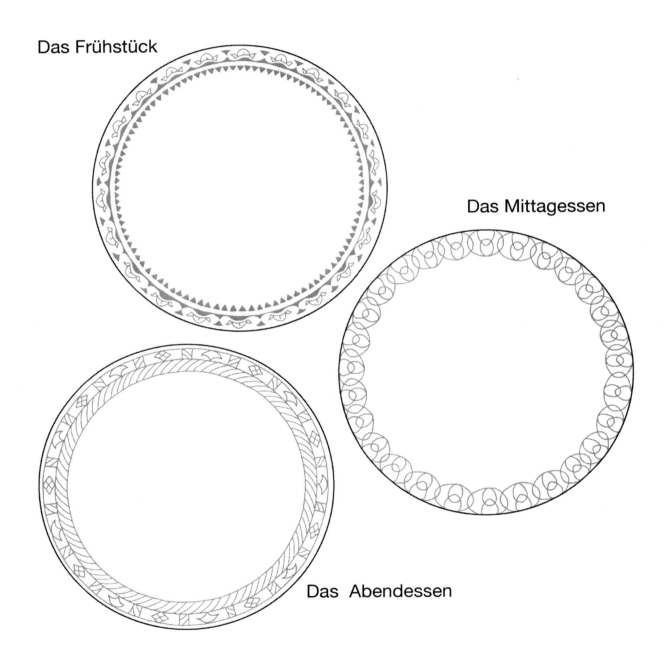

Das Frühstück

Das Mittagessen

Das Abendessen

Extension activity

Sketch typical British meals and compare them to your German meals. Which would you prefer to eat? Can you explain why?

Ostern
Easter

Background information

Good Friday (*Karfreitag*) is a public holiday in Germany. Everything is closed and the church bells stop chiming until mass on Easter Sunday. In some Catholic areas, people go through towns and villages with rattles to make up for the bells not chiming! Good Friday is one of the three 'Quiet Holidays' during the year. Drinking and dancing is not allowed on this day, so all pubs and clubs have to close for 24 hours from midnight the day before.

Easter Sunday (*Ostersonntag*) is also a public holiday. Once again, everything is closed. The bells start chiming again and a new Easter candle will be lit for the first time. The cross, which has been veiled, will be uncovered and all decoration will be restored to the altar. Easter Monday (*Ostermontag*) is also a public holiday, spent with friends and family.

Some of the biggest events on Easter Saturday are the *Osterfeuer* (Easter fires). Huge bonfires are lit in many German cities (especially in northern Germany) and people gather to celebrate. This tradition comes from an old Germanic celebration marking the beginning of spring. The fire is supposed to drive away bad spirits.

Easter in Germany, as in many countries, also means Easter eggs! Another tradition is Easter egg trees, which are almost as prevalent as Christmas trees at Christmas time. People decorate trees and branches with colourful wooden, plastic or blown eggs and put pictures of the Easter bunny in their windows.

Easter egg hunts are also popular across Germany. On Easter Sunday children look for hidden 'Easter nests', little baskets filled with artificial grass (made of paper), and chocolate Easter eggs and bunnies or little presents. Children are told that the Easter bunny has hidden the nests for them.

In some areas children play *Eiertrudeln*, rolling eggs down a hill to see which one reaches the bottom first. Other Easter games are:

Eierbowling	Bowling with hard boiled eggs.
Eierkampf	Hitting each others hard boiled eggs together, the first one to crack loses!
Löffelrennen	Egg and spoon race.

Easter food

On *Gründonnerstag* (Green Thursday), the Thursday before Good Friday, people traditionally eat something green. A popular dish is 'Seven Herb Soup' served with fresh bread. On Karfreitag (Good Friday) a fish dinner is traditional.

People often eat a special Easter breakfast on Sunday morning (*Ostersonntag*) together with family and friends. Traditional foods are coloured hard boiled eggs, smoked ham, braided sweet yeast buns and Easter lambs made out of sponge cake. Quite often the food is consecrated at a special Easter church service very early on Easter morning. For Easter Sunday dinner, lamb is the most popular dish.

Teaching activities

◆ Make some Easter cards or posters (see words in *Schlüsselwörter* box).

Words for your Easter card	
Fröliche Ostern	Happy Easter
Lieber …	Dear… (boy)
Liebe …	Dear… (girl)
mit Liebe von	Love from

◆ Design *Die Ostereiersuche* – an Easter egg hunt game (see page 37).

◆ Make a treasure map. Write instructions in German for how to find the eggs.

Links	left
Rechts	right
Geradeaus	straight on

◆ Hold a 'Decorate an Egg' competition (use either hard boiled eggs or pictures of eggs).

◆ Children could use the guided sheet on page 38 to compare Easter traditions in Britain and Germany.

Schlüsselwörter	
Fröhliche Ostern	Happy Easter
das Osterei	Easter egg
der Osterhase	Easter bunny
das Küken	a chick
das Lamm	a lamb
die Kirche	a church
Lieber …	Dear … (boy)
Liebe …	Dear … (girl)
Mit Liebe von	Love from
Möchtest du spielen?	Would you like to play?
Du bist an der Reihe.	Your turn.
Ich bin an der Reihe.	My turn.
Du hast gewonnen.	You win.
Ich habe gewonnen.	I win.
Anfang	start
Ziel	finish
Würfeln	throw the dice
einmal aussetzen	miss a turn
Rücke X Felder vor.	move forward X spaces.
Gehe X Felder zurück.	move back X spaces.
Karfreitag	Good Friday
Ostersonntag	Easter Sunday
Ostermontag	Easter Monday
Gründonnerstag	Green Thursday
Osterfeuer	Easter fires
Eiertrudeln	egg rolling
Eierbowling	egg bowling
Eierkampf	egg cracking
Löffelrennen	egg and spoon race

German Festivals and Traditions
© *Nicolette Hannam, Michelle Williams and Brilliant Publications*

Design 'Die Ostereiersuche' – an Easter Egg Hunt game

Design an Easter Egg Hunt game and play it with a friend. See if you can play speaking just in German! These words and phrases will help you:

Would you like to play?	Möchtest du spielen?
Your turn.	Du bist an der Reihe.
My turn.	Ich bin an der Reihe.
You win.	Du hast gewonnen.
I win.	Ich habe gewonnen.
Start.	Anfang.
Finish.	Ziel.
Miss a turn.	Aussetzen.
Throw the dice.	Würfeln.
Move forward 3 spaces.	Rücke 3 Felder vor.
Move back 3 spaces.	Gehe 3 Felder zurück.

Ostern

Name: Datum:

I understand how Easter is celebrated in Germany.

Compare and contrast Easter in Germany. Write two lists with the similarities and differences:

Similarities	Differences

How do you celebrate Easter?
If you don't celebrate Easter, write about a different festival.

Extension activity

Use the Internet to find out some more information about how Easter is celebrated in different countries.

German Festivals and Traditions
© Nicolette Hannam, Michelle Williams and Brilliant Publications

Erster April

1st April/April Fool's Day

Background information

Some evidence suggests that April Fool's Day originates from Germany. Credit is given to Gabriel Hoffmann who lived in Damstadt in the 1860s. There is also evidence to suggest that a similar day existed in Roman times, although it was then celebrated on New Year's Day. In Germany, as in many European countries, the 1st of April is the day on which practical jokes can be played on each other until twelve noon. After that it is believed to bring you bad luck if you play a joke on someone. Usually the newspapers, TV and radio stations will also join in to set up a hoax. There have been some very elaborate hoaxes with many people fooled! In Germany an April Fool's joke is known as an *Aprilscherz*. If you fool somebody you say, 'Jemanden in den April schicken', which means, literally, 'to send someone into April'. You say 'April, April' when you have successfully tricked someone.

April Fool's Day is illegal in the Peoples Republic of China, Venezuela, Trinidad and Tobago, Alaska, Cuba and Bolivia.

Here is a Germany 'Klopf Klopf Witz' (knock, knock joke).

Klopf, klopf.	*Knock, knock.*
Wer ist da?	*Who's there?*
Tom.	*Tom.*
Tom wer?	*Tom who?*
Tom Ate.	*Tomato.*

Teaching activities

◆ Can you make up any of your own jokes in German?

◆ Write an acrostic poem about jokes and tricks using 'April Fool' as the title.

◆ Make a poster of your favourite jokes.

◆ Ask each member of your family for their favourite joke and write it down to add to a class anthology.

◆ Tell the class some jokes, in English. Others can score them out of ten for content and delivery.

◆ Children can use the guided sheet on page 40 to compare April Fool's Day in Britain and Germany.

Schlüsselwörter

der Aprilscherz	April Fool's joke
Erster April	1st April
Jemanden in den April schicken.	To send someone into April.
Klopf, Klopf	knock, knock
ein Witz	a joke
Wer ist da?	Who's there?
Wer?	Who?
die Tomate	tomato

Erster April

Name: Datum:

I have learned about April Fool's Day in Germany.

Write down at least three facts about April Fool's Day in Germany:

Describe a good April Fool's Day trick below. You could write it in the form of a diary or a newspaper report.

Extension activity

◆ Can you make up your own 'Klopf, Klopf' joke in German? Ask your teacher for help.

Tag der Arbeit
May Day/Labour Day

Background information

In many countries May Day (*Maifeiertag*) is synonymous with Labour Day which celebrates the social and economic achievements of the labour movement. Historically, this widespread custom was inspired by events in the United States. In 1889, in Paris, a congress of world socialist parties was held. The people attending this conference voted to support workers on strike in the United States who were demanding an eight hour working day. So, in many countries in the world, May 1st became an official holiday.

In Austria and many parts of Germany (especially in the south), the tradition of raising a maypole (*der Maibaum*) on 1st May serves to welcome spring. Similar maypole festivities are held in England, Finland, Sweden and the Czech Republic.

In German the *Maibaum* literally translates as 'May tree'. This reflects the custom of placing a small pine tree on top of the Maypole. On the 1st May, villages put up a maypole, usually a tall birch or pine tree. The maypole is then decorated. The night before it is guarded, as it is customary to try to steal the maypole from neighbouring villages!

Both men and women hold a ribbon each and weave in and out of each other around the maypole. People play music and sing around the maypole as they watch the dancers. On a leap year it is traditional for only the women to dance around the maypole. In Bavaria, they hold maypole climbing contests, with lots of beer as the main prize. It is made particularly difficult as the chosen tree trunk is shaved of any bark and polished! The contests are known as *Maibaumkraxeln*.

May Day itself is celebrated with big street parties and fairs. People meet and eat *Bratwurst* (a type of sausage – see page 30) and drink *Bier*. There may be a ceremony in which a May Queen is chosen and crowned.

In many rural regions people would have had a bonfire and a party the night before as well. Events on this evening are called *Tanz in den Mai* (Dance into May), and quite often there is live music. This night is also known for the witches who gather at the summit of a certain mountain, the *Blocksberg* (also called the *Blocken*), to dance and celebrate!

In Western Germany, a lucky girl may find a small tree decorated with streamers or ribbons on her doorstep, left there by a love interest. May is traditionally known as the *Wonnemonat*, the month of lovers, and is the most popular month in which to hold your wedding.

Teaching activities

◆ How do the German people celebrate public holidays? Write some similarities and differences between how we celebrate and how German people celebrate.

◆ Girls could describe their dream wedding!

◆ Children could make up a song about May.

◆ You could nominate and dress a May Queen in your class.

◆ You could hold a climbing contest, or a similar contest of strength.

◆ Children could draw and label the climbing contest. They could also make a poster celebrating an imaginary winner.

◆ You could hot seat the May Queen, or the winner of the climbing competition.

◆ Children could talk about great street parties that they have attended.

◆ Design a poster for a May Day party. (See the *Schlüsselwörter* box for useful vocabulary.)

◆ Children could use the guided sheet on page 43 to plan a May Day celebration.

Schlüsselwörter

der Maibaum	maypole
Tanzen	dancing
Klettern	climbing
das Essen	food
die Getränke	drink
das Bier	beer
die Wurst	sausage
das Datum	date
die Uhrzeit	time
die Maikönigin	May Queen
Maibaumkraxeln	May Pole climbing
der Wonnemonat	month of lovers

German Festivals and Traditions
© Nicolette Hannam, Michelle Williams and Brilliant Publications

Tag der Arbeit

Name: Datum:

I understand how and why May Day is celebrated in Germany.

When is 'May Day' in Germany?

Draw a mind map below planning a May Day party. Give details of activities, food, people invited, and so on.

Extension activity

Design a maypole. Look on the Internet for some ideas.

Muttertag

Mother's Day

Background information

Muttertag was first observed in Germany in 1922 and was declared an official German holiday in 1933. It takes place on the second Sunday in May, except when this date is *Pfingstsonntag* (Pentecost). Then it is moved to the first Sunday in May. So in Germany, Mother's Day is in May, not March!

During the Hitler regime, there was a medal, *das Mutterkreuz* in bronze, silver and gold which was awarded to mothers who produced children for the Vaterland. To get a gold medal, you had to have eight or more children! After World War II and the founding of the German republic (*Bundesrepublik*), Mother's Day became an opportunity for people to honour their own mothers. Interestingly, in Eastern Germany (DDR), Mother's Day was not celebrated. Instead, 'International Women's Day' (*Internationaler Frauentag*) was observed on March 8th.

Today *Muttertag* in Germany is celebrated in the same way as we celebrate, giving cards, flowers and presents. Families try to get together for a special meal. Very traditional Germans will wear a white carnation in a jacket buttonhole in remembrance of a mother passed on, or a coloured carnation for a mother still living.

Teaching activities

◆ Make a Mother's Day card. (See the *Schlüsselwörter* box for useful words.)

◆ Make a list of celebrity mums! Do you know any German celebrity mums?

◆ Write an acrostic poem with the title 'Meine Mutter'.

◆ Draw and describe your mum. How much can you label in German?

◆ Revise names of family members in German.

◆ Draw the family tree of your favourite character, for example Bart Simpson.

◆ Use the photocopiable sheet on page 45 to describe an ideal Mother's Day.

◆ Design a medal for your mum.

Schlüsselwörter	
Alles Gute zum Muttertag	Happy Mother's Day
Liebe Mutti	Dear Mum
Ich liebe dich	I love you
Liebe	Dear (girl)
mit Liebe von	love from
Meine Mutter ist …	My mum is ….
geduldig	patient
nett	nice
hilfsbereit	helpful
schön	beautiful
komisch	funny
intelligent	intelligent

German Festivals and Traditions
© Nicolette Hannam, Michelle Williams and Brilliant Publications

Muttertag

Name: Datum:

I understand how and why Mother's Day is celebrated in Germany.

> When is Mother's Day celebrated in Germany?

> How is Mother's Day celebrated in Germany?

> Describe an ideal Mother's Day below. Where could you go? What could you do? How could you make your mum feel special?

Extension activity

Can you make up a Mother's Day rhyme or poem in German?

Sommersonnenwende

Summer Solstice

Background information

The 21st of June is the longest day of the year. In Germany this day is celebrated with bonfires and fireworks. People drink *Bier* and eat *Bratwurst* and traditionally the Mayor gives a short speech. The bonfire is lit by local children using torches, usually at about 7pm and fires are left burning throughout the night. These fires are also often associated with the day of Saint Johannes (Saint John the Baptist) on 24th of June, so they are called *Johannisfeuer*.

In the United Kingdom it is a time associated with magic, fairies and witches. Bonfires are also lit, traditionally in an attempt to strengthen the Sun. Many people travel to Stonehenge in Dorset, a ring of huge stones dating back almost 5000 years. On Midsummer Day, at sunrise, the sun shines directly in the middle of the circle of stones.

Teaching activities

◆ Draw a picture of a bonfire party.

◆ Design a German invite to a bonfire party. Use the invitation template on page 17.

◆ What type of food and drink would be on offer at a British bonfire party? How does it compare to German party food?

◆ Research Stonehenge on the Internet.

◆ Plan your own party with a sunshine theme. Think of costumes, invites, food and so on.

◆ Illustrate the following words associated with *Sommersonnenwende*:

die Sonne	sun
das Feuer	bonfire
das Feuerwerk	fireworks
die Fee	fairy
die Hexe	witch
die Zauberei	magic

◆ Children could use the photocopiable guided sheet on page 47 to record their understanding of when and how *Sommersonnenwende* is celebrated in Germany.

Schlüsselwörter

die Sonne	sun
das Feuer	fire
das Feuerwerk	fireworks
die Fee	fairy
die Hexe	witch
die Zauberei	magic

Sommersonnenwende

Name: Datum:

I have learned about how German people celebrate *Sommersonnenwende*.

What does the *Sommersonnenwende* celebrate? When is it?

How is the *Sommersonnenwende* celebrated?

Extension activity

Imagine that you have been to a Sommersonnenwende bonfire party. Write a postcard to a friend describing how you celebrated. Include what you did and what you ate and drank.

Viel Glück zum Geburtstag

Happy Birthday

Background information

In Germany, when it is your birthday, all your family gathers together to wish you a Happy Birthday, which in German is *Viel Glück zum Geburtstag!*.

On the cake, you have candles according to your age. Then, all the family sings *Zum Geburtstag viel Glück* – 'Happy Birthday to you!' They use the same tune as we do.

Here are the words in German:

Zum Geburtstag viel Glück
Zum Geburtstag viel Glück
Zum Geburtstag lieber/liebe (name)
Zum Geburtstag viel Glück.

After eating the cake, your family gives you presents and cards. In Germany children aren't given homework or chores on their birthday.

It is considered bad luck to wish someone a 'Happy Birthday' or give a card or present before the actual day. So, just to be on the safe side, many Germans wait until after the day has passed to send cards and presents.

Some popular German names

Boy's names	Girl's names
Lucas	Anna
Leon	Leoni
Luka	Lea
Timm	Lena
Jonas	Michaela
Max	Emilie
Niklas	Lilli

Personalausweis

It is compulsory for all German citizens aged 16 or older to possess either a *Personalausweis* (identity card) or a passport, but not to carry it. The *Personalausweis* can be used instead of a passport when travelling within the European Union. It is a plastic ID card which contains, on the front side, name, date and place of birth, nationality, date of expiration, signature and photo. On the reverse side are the address, height, colour of eyes, issuing authority and date of issue.

Teaching activities

◆ Make a birthday card or party invitation.

◆ Design your own ID card (*Personalausweis*), with the following information on it:

Name:	Name
Geburtstag:	Birthday
Alter:	Age
Wohnort:	Where you live
Familie:	Family
Haare:	Hair
Augen:	Eyes
Größe:	Height
Hobbys:	Hobbies

◆ Sing *Zum Geburtstag viel Glück* – to the tune of 'Happy Birthday to You':

◆ Do a birthday survey (*Umfrage*) to find out in which month people in your class have their birthday.

Wann hast du Geburtstag?
Mein Geburtstag ist am …

Name	Geburtstag
Frau Williams	20. Juni
Hans	17. April

◆ Children could use the guided sheet on page 50 to compare traditional birthday celebrations in Germany and Britain.

Schlüsselwörter

der Personalausweis	ID card
der Name	name
der Geburtstag	birthday
das Alter	age
der Wohnort	where you live
die Familie	family
die Haare	hair
die Augen	eyes
die Größe	height
die Hobbys	hobbies
Viel Glück zum Geburtstag	Happy Birthday
eine Umfrage	a survey
Wann hast du Geburtstag?	When is your birthday?
Mein Geburtstag ist am …	My birthday is …

Viel Glück zum Geburtstag

Name: Datum:

I understand how birthdays are celebrated in Germany.

If you were in Germany and it was your birthday, how would you celebrate?

Draw some presents you would like to receive and use a German dictionary to help you label them.

Extension activity

Write a letter to a real or imaginary German friend telling him or her how you celebrate your birthday.

German Festivals and Traditions
© Nicolette Hannam, Michelle Williams and Brilliant Publications

German festivals

Background information

Summer in Germany is festival time. There are many types of festival that bring people together and entertain them. They are usually outside, with outdoor cafes. There is often free music as entertainment. There are festivals for wine and beer, food festivals, fairgrounds and even a hot air balloon festival.

The Hamburg Dom is one of the most famous festivals, so popular that it now happens three times a year, in spring, summer and winter. It takes place on a large field very near the centre of Hamburg. The summer Dom has a cowboy theme, and the winter Dom has a magical and medieval theme. Each Dom is opened by three cannon salutes by a member of the Hamburg senate. The tradition dates back to the fourteenth century when St Mary's Cathedral (Dom in German) offered refuge to traders, craftsmen and travelling musicians.

The Rhine in Flames takes place over five summer nights, one in July. You can enjoy an amazing firework display from the banks of the Rhine or onboard a boat. Castles and towers are lit by the huge amount of fireworks in the sky. Illuminated ships form a procession along the river. People enjoy the spectacle with some food and some wine.

There are many other festivals, many of them free. There is the Rheinkultur Bonn, the Schlagermove pop music festival, Zeltfestival in Hamburg and Das Fest in Karlsruhe. The entertainment is enjoyed by many people, including tourists.

Teaching activities

◆ Children could use the Internet to research and produce a mind map of all the different festivals in Germany.

◆ Children could write a diary entry of a trip to one of the festivals.

◆ Children could design posters advertising one of the festivals.

◆ Children could use the photocopiable sheet on page 52 to design a British festival.

◆ Children could draw a plan of a German festival. They could detail what is available in each tent.

◆ Drawing floor plans of the festivals could be linked to co-ordinate work in maths.

◆ Children could interview each other, pretending they have been to a festival.

Schlüsselwörter	
das Fest	festival
das Zelt	tent
das Essen	food
das Getränk	drink
die Musik	music
der Jahrmarkt	funfair

German festivals

Name: Datum:

I understand the cultural importance of a festival.

Use this sheet to plan a festival in Britain. The food, drink and activities on offer must represent British culture.

Where will your festival take place?

Draw a floor plan below. Write on each tent what will be available.

How does your festival represent Britain?

Extension activity
What do you know about Britain? Compile a fact file.

German symbols

German flag

The German flag is divided horizontally into thirds, coloured black, red and yellow. The colours black, red and yellow (gold) have been associated with Germany since the middle ages, but the current German flag colours can be traced back to the uniforms soldiers wore in the Napoleonic Wars which were black coats with red braid and gold buttons.

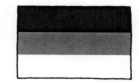

Coat-of-Arms (Bundeswappen)

The German coat of arms uses the colours of the German flag, and depicts an eagle. The Romans were the first to use the image of an eagle. There have been many variations of the design over the years, due to political and military reasons. The current design dates from 1926, and was designed by Tobias Schwab. It can now be found on coins, stamps and official letter heads.

Germania

Germania is the personification of German people. It depicts a woman with long, reddish blonde hair. She wears a crown and holds a sword, known as Joyeuse. She wears armour and holds a medieval style shield with the eagle on it. The name of the country 'Germany' derives from Germania.

Liberty Bell

The Liberty Bell hangs in the tower of Berlin's city hall and was a gift from America to the city of Berlin in 1950. It weighs ten tonnes. It is a symbol of the fight for freedom and represents a stand against communism in Europe. It is rung every day at noon, and at midnight on Christmas Eve and New Year's Eve.

The Brandenburg Gate

The Brandenburg Gate has evolved from a symbol of division into a symbol of unity. During the time when Germany was divided, the Gate was part of the wall that divided East and West Berlin and was blocked up.

The Gate was originally commissioned by Friedrich Wilhelm II as a symbol of peace and was completed in 1791. The architect, Carl Gotthard Langhans, modelled the design on the entrance to the Acropolis in Athens. Its design has remained essentially unchanged since then, although it suffered damage and various decorations were taken off and then replaced during the Napoleonic Wars and World War II.

Until August 1961 vehicles and pedestrians could travel freely through the gate. Then the Berlin Wall was erected (see Tag der Deutschen Einheit, pages 69–70). In November 1989 the Wall came down and people could once again travel through the Brandenburg Gate. The Gate is now again closed for vehicle traffic, and much of the surrounding area has been turned into a cobblestone pedestrian zone. The Brandenburg Gate is a popular tourist site and now appears on Euro coins.

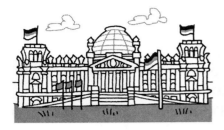

Der Reichstag

Der Reichstag is the German parliament. It was built between 1884 and 1894, but suffered a lot of damage during World War II. It was rebuilt after reunification and is now well known for its glass dome at the top of the building. The dome is open to visitors and has a 360-degree view of the city of Berlin. The main hall of the parliament below can also be seen from the dome.

German cars

Germany has an excellent reputation for designing and manufacturing cars, including Mercedes Benz, Audi, Volkswagen, Porsche and BMW. They also make the Maybach, a very expensive, high quality car.

Teaching activities

◆ Discuss symbols in The United Kingdom (see box).

◆ Ask the children if they know any symbols for local sports teams. They could design one for a school team.

◆ Children could investigate and draw the car symbols. Or they could design their own.

◆ Use the photocopiable sheet on page 55 to design a British coat of arms. You may want to download a colour version from the Internet. The colours are as follows:

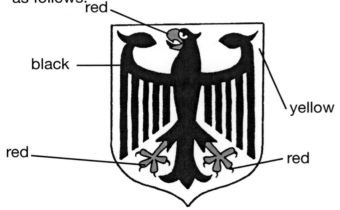

red
black
red
yellow
red

Symbols of the United Kingdom

The Union Jack, and each country's flag within it (see below)

England
Symbols: the three lions, red rose (appears on the England Rugby Team kit), oak tree
Patron saint: St George (23rd April)
Flag: the red cross (cross of St George)

Scotland
Symbols: the thistle, bagpipes, tartan kilts
Patron saint: St Andrew (30th November)
Flag: white diagonal cross (called a saltire) on a blue background (cross of St Andrew)

Northern Ireland
Symbols: shamrock, harp, Celtic cross
Patron saint: St Patrick (17th March)
Flag: red diagonal cross (saltire) on a white background (cross of St Patrick)

Wales
Symbols: leeks, daffodils, red dragon.
Patron saint: St David (1st March)
Flag: red dragon on a white (top) and green (bottom) background

You could also discuss The Royal Family.

◆ Children could be introduced to Makaton, a system for communicating with disabled people which uses symbols.

◆ Each child could colour the German flag onto a sheet of paper. These could be stapled together onto string across the classroom to make a banner.

◆ Learn about flags around the world. Draw and colour some.

German Festivals and Traditions
© Nicolette Hannam, Michelle Williams and Brilliant Publications

German symbols

Name: Datum:

I can recognize some German symbols.

Look carefully at this picture of the German coat of arms. Sketch and colour it in the next box.

Now design a coat of arms for Britain. Write a brief description of it as well.

Extension activity

Design a coat of arms for your school or your family.

Planning a holiday

Background information

Germany is a large country in the centre of Europe. With over 80 million inhabitants, it has the largest population in Europe. It shares borders with France, Belgium, Holland, Denmark, Luxembourg, Austria, Switzerland, Poland and the Czech Republic. It is also bordered by the North and Baltic Seas. The country itself has a wide cultural mix. Over 2 million people there originally came from Turkey. Other nationalities that live in Germany include Polish, Italian and Greek.

The capital of Germany is Berlin, in the north-east. It lies on the banks of the rivers Spree and Havel. Much of the city has been renovated following reunification in 1990. For more information on the Reichstag (the German parliament building) and the Brandenburg Gate see pages 54–55. Berlin hosted the 1936 Olympic Games and the 2006 FIFA World Cup Final.

The highest mountain in Germany is the Zugspitze at 2962 m on the German/Austrian border. The Rhine, one of the longest and most important rivers in Europe, runs through Germany. The Rhine (or Rhein, as it is known in Germany) starts in the Alps in Switzerland and flows through Germany, France and the Netherlands, before emptying into the North Sea. In all it is 1320km long.

Germany can offer many types of holiday – coastal, lakes, busy cities, mountains and so on. They have a huge motorway system (the Autobahn) which covers the whole country and links Germany to the rest of Europe. The Bavarian Alps are in the south of Germany. There are many lakes including Lake Constance and Lake Muritz. The Black Forest in the south-west is popular with British tourists.

Travelling to Germany

We can travel to Germany by ferry, aeroplane or train. Many people choose to drive to a ferry port and travel by boat so that they have their own car whilst they are abroad. The easiest route to Germany is to travel by ferry to Holland (Harwich to Hook of Holland) and drive to Germany from there. People can eat, sleep or even go to the cinema on a ferry. Flying to Germany is easy and quite affordable now. Popular British airports are London Heathrow, Gatwick, Stansted or Leeds Bradford. You can fly to almost every major city in Germany (Munich, Frankfurt, Dusseldorf, Berlin, Cologne and Hamburg) depending on which airline you choose.

Since 1994 you can travel to Europe by train. The Eurotunnel is a twin tunnel built under the English Channel, linking Folkestone in England to Calais in France. You can drive on and stay in your car for the 35 minute journey. Alternatively, Eurostar trains leave for Brussels (in Belgium) from St Pancreas International Station in London several times a day, travelling through the tunnel. In Brussels you can transfer to high-speed trains travelling to many locations in Germany. The total journey from London to Cologne by train takes approximately five hours.

Where else is German spoken?

German is the official language of Germany, Austria, Luxembourg and Liechtenstein. German is also an official language in Switzerland, where over half of the inhabitants speak it, and in Belgium, where less than 1% of the population speak it. German is also spoken in regions of France, Denmark, Romania, Bosnia, Poland, Italy, the Czech Republic, Poland, Russia and the Ukraine. There are also colonies of German-speakers in the United States, Canada, Brazil and Argentina. Surprisingly there are also quite a few German-speaking people in Namibia. German uses the Latin alphabet with the addition of three letters with diacritics (ä, ü and ö) and one ligature (ß). German dialects are divided into Low German, spoken in the flat northern areas, Upper German, spoken in the mountainous south and Austria and Central German.

Teaching activities

◆ Look at a map of Germany and give the children some key facts about Germany. Make comparisons to the United Kingdom in your discussion. There are many good examples of maps of Germany on the Internet. Discuss main towns, key geographical features and well-known landmarks.

Schlüsselwörter	
der Urlaub	holiday
die Fähre	ferry
der Zug	train
das Flugzeug	aeroplane
das Auto	car
reisen	to travel

◆ The children could plan a holiday to Germany, or another German-speaking country, following your discussion.

◆ The children could work in pairs to draw a Venn diagram, comparing Germany and the United Kingdom.

◆ Children could pretend to be on holiday in Germany and write a postcard home.

◆ Children could plan their dream holiday to a destination of their choice. They need to think about the climate, which languages are spoken there and the activities available. (See guided sheet on page 58.)

◆ Children could write about the best holiday they have ever had and explain why.

◆ Use weather sites on the Internet to compare weather in a locality in Germany, eg in the Bavarian Alps or in Berlin, with that in your locality, over a period of time.

◆ Children could make a poster advertising either Britain or Germany as an excellent holiday destination. They should use a range of persuasive techniques (link to Literacy work).

◆ More able pupils could highlight all the places on a world map where German is spoken.

◆ Do a survey to find out which other languages are spoken in the school. Locate the country/ countries where these languages are spoken using maps, atlases and globes.

◆ Talk to the children about which other languages they would like to learn and why.

Planning a holiday

Name: Datum:

I can plan a trip.

Where are you travelling from?

Which mode(s) of transport will you use?

train ☐   bus ☐
aeroplane ☐   boat/ferry ☐
car ☐   walk ☐
bike ☐   other ☐

Where are you travelling to?

Where will you stay? What type of accommodation?

What will you do on your trip? Draw and describe some activities.

Extension activity

Is your holiday to a popular tourist destination? Explain your answer.

German Festivals and Traditions
© Nicolette Hannam, Michelle Williams and Brilliant Publications

How is German culture incorporated into our everyday life?

Background information

Due to the amount of travelling that takes place across and around the world, the cultures of different countries can be transferred to new places more easily. Some people immigrate to different countries and take traditions with them. Others bring back ideas from travels and holidays.

Popular songs and films demonstrate different cultures and influence audiences. Many people travel as part of their job, and may return to places for holidays. Television programmes show us places and recipes we have never seen before, and inspire us to try new things.

Large supermarkets are great places to examine the influence of different cultures through the foods that are sold. German beer is popular and *Bratwurst* can often be bought fresh from larger stores.

Teaching activities

◆ Use the guided sheet on page 60 to look at similarities and differences between two localities, perhaps Germany and the United Kingdom. Develop this into a discussion on cultural diversity.

◆ Discuss German influences on life in the United Kingdom. Topics could include language, food, drink, music, fashion and so on.

Comparing cultures

Name: Datum:

I can compare two countries.

Name	Flag
Population	
Size	
Languages spoken	
Famous landmarks	Major cities/towns
Famous food	Additional information

Name	Flag
Population	
Size	
Languages spoken	
Famous landmarks	Major cities/towns
Famous food	Additional information

German Festivals and Traditions
© Nicolette Hannam, Michelle Williams and Brilliant Publications

A typical school day in Germany

Background information

Most children start pre-school in a *Kindergarten*, between the ages of two and six. Starting primary school is a big occasion in Germany. Children are given a *Schultüte* by family and friends. It is a large cardboard cone filled with sweets and pencil case items for school. Many children receive a *Füller*, a fountain pen, which they will write with throughout their school life. After the child's first day at school relatives and family call round to congratulate them and enjoy coffee and cake together.

Children start primary school (*die Grundschule*) at the age of six. After that, at the age of ten, they have a choice of schools: *Gymnasium*, *Hauptschule* and *Realschule*.
Gifted children are encouraged to attend *Gymnasium*, which prepares them for university. Intermediate children can attend *Realschule* which combines practical subjects with academic classes. Less able pupils attend *Hauptschule* which offers slower paced instruction in core areas, along with vocational training. It leads to apprenticeship training for specific jobs. In some German States, pupils are able to attend a *Gesamtschule* (comprehensive school), which offers a combination of all three choices.

School starts at around 8am and finishes around 1–2pm. Children will then usually go home for a hot lunch. They may have already snacked on fruit or sandwiches in the short breaks between their school sessions. Traditionally lunch (*Mittagessen*) was the main meal of the day. In modern times people tend to eat in the evenings, to fit around working life. Depending on their age, and which school they go to, on certain days children may have one or two more lessons in the afternoon.

Children do not wear uniform in German schools. They are given a lot of homework and some complain of the pressure of school (*der Schulstress*). Some schools in Germany have lessons on Saturday mornings. Most classes will go on at least one school trip a year (*eine Klassenfahrt*), often a residential trip. Children have a good choice of clubs outside of school hours (*die Arbeitsgemeinschaft*) including music, sport and drama.

Teaching activities

◆ Children could think about their first day at school in a new school year. How did they feel? What did they do?

◆ You could teach the German names for some school subjects and children could design a timetable, taking into account the different timings. They could then compare this to their own timetable.

◆ You could display your class timetable in German and ask children which lessons they have had, or will have next, eg 'Which lesson do you have in the morning?' 'Which lesson do you have after this one?' 'Which lesson do you have on Friday afternoon?' *'Was ist dein Lieblingsfach?'*

◆ Children could design a brochure to welcome newcomers to their year group next September.

◆ Children could decorate a typical menu for a German child, drawing a picture of each dish (see page 63). The audience could be German children. More able children could carefully write out the German onto a plain sheet and decorate.

Schlüsselwörter	
der Kindergarten	nursery
die Grundschule	primary school
die Hauptschule	vocational secon-day school
die Realschule	general secondary school
die Gymnasium	grammar school
die Gesamtschule	comprehensive school
das Mittagessen	lunch
der Schulstress	pressure of school
eine Klassenfahrt	school trip
die Arbeitgemeinschaft	after school clubs
die Mathe	Maths
die Naturwissenschaft	Science
das Deutsch	German
das English	English
die Kunst	Art
die Geschichte	History
die Erdkunde	Geography
die Musik	Music
der Sport	PE
das Werken	Design and technology
die Informatik	ICT

Speisekarte

Hauptspeise	**Main course**
Kartoffelsalat mit Frikadellen	Potato salad with meatballs
Grüne Bohnen	Green beans
Möhren	Carrots
Nachtisch	**Dessert**
Apfelpfannkuchen	Apple pancakes

◆ Children could draw or write their meal, and compare it with the German meal.

◆ Children could revise the German names of the fruit and vegetables they have learned as a link to healthy eating. They could draw and label them.

◆ Children could list food they do and do not like.

A typical German lunch

Name: Datum:

I can describe a typical German lunch:

Mittagessen

Hauptspeise

Kartoffelsalat mit Frikadellen

Grüne Bohnen

Möhren

Nachtisch

Apfelpfannkuchen

Extension activities

What did you have for your lunch today?

Which lunch would you prefer? Why?

Comparing pastimes and everyday life

Background information

German children have similar hobbies to British children. Everyday life is also very similar. School life may differ slightly (eg, children do not wear uniform to school). Food and drink is different, although many staple ingredients remain the same. The most beneficial way to compare everyday life is to show video clips of German children to begin discussions. It will most likely develop into a discussion about stereotypes and their inaccuracies (see also Challenging stereotypes, pages 78–79).

Teaching activities

◆ Children could compare their own pastimes/hobbies with German children, using the guided sheet on page 65. They will find that they are very similar.

◆ Discuss similarities and differences in everyday life between Germany and the United Kingdom.

◆ Children could mime activities and say what they are doing in German. Alternatively, you could play a game of Simon sagt (Simon Says).

◆ Try this hot potato activity. Give each table a large sheet of paper. Each table has 2 minutes to write as much as they know about the lives of German and English children. Pass the sheets around (giving 2 minutes for each sheet), until each table has written on every sheet. Share and discuss findings.

◆ Children could compile a list of questions they would like to ask a German person.

◆ If possible, invite a native speaker in to talk about their hobbies as a child.

◆ Children could write a postcard home from Germany detailing the activities they have done, in German.

Schlüsselwörter

das Hobby	hobby
Ich spiele …	I play …
Klavier	piano
Violine	violin
Flöte	flute
Gitarre	guitar
Ich spiele …	I play …
Fußball	football
Basketball	basketball
Rugby	rugby
Volleyball	volleyball
Hockey	hockey
Golf	golf
Playstation	playstation
Computerspiele	computer games
Ich fahre Rad	I cycle
Ich mache Gymnastik	I do gymnastics
Ich mache Judo	I do judo
Ich mache Liechtathletik	I do athletics
Ich mache Karate	I do karate
Ich gehe Reiten	I go horse riding
Ich gehe Schwimmen	I go swimming
Ich gehe Segeln	I go sailing

German Festivals and Traditions
© Nicolette Hannam, Michelle Williams and Brilliant Publications

Comparing pastimes

Nom: Date:

I can compare children's pastimes in Britain and Germany.

Look at the information about a child in German. Then complete the box below, in the same style, with information about yourself.

Name	Michael	Self-portrait
Date of birth	7.Januar 1997	
Place of birth	München	
Favourite food	Bonbons	**Hobbies** — Reiten (horse riding) / Segeln (sailing) / Schwimmen (swimming) / Fußball (football)
Favourite drink	Limonade	

Name		Self-portrait
Date of birth		
Place of birth		
Favourite food		**Hobbies**
Favourite drink		

German wine

Background

German wine is mainly produced in the southwest of the country, along the river Rhine. The oldest plantations date back to the Roman era and Germany today is the ninth largest wine-producing country. Germany produces many types of wines: dry and sweet white wines, rosé wines, red wines and sparkling wines called 'Sekt.' In Britain, we are most familiar with 'Liebfraumilch' and 'Riesling' wines.

Moselle Wine Festival

There are hundreds of wine harvest celebrations which range from small parties to large open air festivals. These *Weinfeste* date back hundreds of years and you can enjoy German food, wine, culture and music at them. The Moselle Wine Festival takes place in Bernkastel-Kues, a village near Trier during the first week in September. A famous attraction at this time is the town fountain which spews Moselle wine!

Teaching activities

◆ Look out for signs and posters promoting Moselle wine in September.

◆ Design your own wine label using the name of your school, for example, 'Schloss Battyeford.'

◆ Use the Internet to find out more about the origins of wine making.

◆ Search for some other famous German wines and vineyards.

Schlüsselwörter

der Rotwein	red wine
der Weißwein	white wine
eine Flasche	a bottle
ein Etikett	a label
die Trauben	grapes
ein Weinberg	a vineyard
das Weinfeste	wine festival
das Schloss	castle

German Festivals and Traditions
© Nicolette Hannam, Michelle Williams and Brilliant Publications

Halloween

Halloween

Background information

Halloween began in the British Isles as a festival called Samhain. It was believed that on this day spirits rose from the dead. So people wore masks to scare bad spirits away. Centuries later, in the 1840s, Halloween found its way to America with the Irish immigrants. Over time, it developed into the children's festival that we now know.

Halloween is not a traditional German holiday. But the Germans began to hear about it from tourists, and in their English lessons. German children prefer to have a themed party, rather than go trick or treating. They enjoy dressing up in costumes, and there are now many shops and places on the Internet where you can buy Halloween costumes and decorations.

Teaching Activities

◆ Use flashcards to teach the children Halloween-related vocabulary. Children could then use cards made from page 68 to play Pelmanism (Pairs) or Snap to reinforce the vocabulary.

◆ Children could write a German Halloween word each and draw a picture to match it.

◆ Link to Literacy – children could write a spooky Halloween story.

◆ Anagrams – you could muddle up the letters of the words for children to unscramble.

◆ Write a recount (link to Literacy) about Trick or Treating.

◆ Design your own spooky costume.

◆ Put the spooky words in alphabetical order.

◆ Design a Halloween poster, and include some spooky German words.

Schlüsselwörter

ein Gespenst	a ghost
ein Schädel	a skull
ein Kostüm	a costume
ein Vampir	a vampire
ein Spukhaus	a haunted house
eine Hexe	a witch
die Süßigkeiten	sweets
ein Skelett	a skeleton
eine Spinne	a spider
ein Zombie	a zombie
ein Kürbis	a pumpkin

Halloween words

ein Gespenst		eine Hexe	
ein Schädel		die Süßigkeiten	
ein Kostüm		ein Skelett	
ein Vampir		eine Spinne	
ein Spukhaus		ein Zombie	

German Festivals and Traditions
© Nicolette Hannam, Michelle Williams and Brilliant Publications

Tag der Deutschen Einheit
German Unity Day

Background information

German Unity Day is a national holiday, celebrated on the 3rd October each year. It marks the day that a reunification treaty was signed in 1990 between East and West Germany.

Following World War II, Germany was divided into four military sectors controlled by France, the United Kingdom, the United States and the Soviet Union. In 1949 the sectors controlled by France, the United Kingdom and the United States became the Federal Republic of Germany (West Germany) and the sector controlled by the Soviet Union became the German Democratic Republic (East Germany). The city of Berlin was split in half.

In 1961 the Berlin Wall was built to stop people from East Berlin defecting to West Berlin. The Wall was 96 miles long and surrounded all of West Berlin. There were eights crossings, all manned by armed guards. The wall became a symbol of the Iron Curtain, the ideological divide between the communist east and the west.

Some families were split from each other by the wall, and many people were cut off from their jobs. West Berliners needed permits to visit East Berlin, which they had to obtain in advance. The only way that East Berliners could cross into West Berlin was if they were old age pensioners, were visiting family for very important matters or needed to cross for professional reasons. Underground trains continued to run although many lines were cut in half or stations shut. One West Berlin route travelled through three stations in East Berlin but could not stop. Foreigners could cross through the infamous Checkpoint Charlie.

After 28 years the wall was knocked down, starting on November 9th 1989 when the East German government announced that the checkpoints would be open. Many adults will remember news footage of ecstatic German people climbing the wall and chipping bits away to keep as souvenirs. Days later industrial machinery was used to complete the task. Germany's unification became official when a treaty was signed on October 3rd 1990.

German Unity Day is the only national holiday in Germany, as all other holidays are administered by individual States. Most people have a day off work and big public celebrations are organized, including speeches by politicians and other leaders, concerts, food and fireworks. Each year a different city hosts the national celebrations. Many mosques in Germany are open to the general public on October 3rd to illustrate the strong identification many Muslims feel with Germany and the role Muslims played in the building of Germany today.

Teaching Activities

◆ This subject could be linked to History and World War II. Children could research Germany and the implications of the division.

◆ Encourage children to ask older family members if they remember the Berlin Wall coming down.

◆ Children could label a map of Europe and learn facts about Germany as it is now.

◆ Children could imagine they are on the Berlin Wall on November 9th 1989. They could write a historical recount.

◆ Children could role play being a news reporter at the Berlin Wall. They could interview some German people. This could be videoed and linked to ICT lessons.

◆ Children could write a diary entry of someone who is affected by the division.

◆ Children could plan activities for celebrating German Unity Day in Germany.

◆ Children could plan a British Day – an imaginary public holiday where people celebrate living in Britain.

German Festivals and Traditions
© Nicolette Hannam, Michelle Williams and Brilliant Publications

Oktoberfest

Background information

The first Oktoberfest was in 1810 and was a public celebration of the wedding of the Crown Prince Ludwig of Bavaria and Princess Theresse of Sachsen-Hildburghausen. The wedding was held on a large meadow in Munich and the citizens of Munich enjoyed horse racing, beer, food and music. Anniversary celebrations have continued every year in Munich, interrupted only during wartime years.

The Oktoberfest is also known as *Wiesn* which is Bavarian for meadow. It begins in mid-September and lasts three weeks until the first week in October. It begins with a procession by brewers and publicans and lots of decorated carts, some pulled by large cart horses. Many people wear regional costumes. Then at 12 noon the Lord Mayor of Munich taps the first barrel of beer and declares the festival open.

Special *Wiesn* beer is brewed for the occasion. It is strong and dark. Beer palaces are set up by the major breweries and there are lots of tents where snacks are sold. Musicians play in many of the tents. There is an amusement park area with a huge variety of rides and games. The enormous fairgrounds have been called *Theresienwiese* after the Princess Therese.

Many people wear traditional Bavarian costume. Men wear *Lederhosen* – short suede leather trousers which are held up by leather braces – along with a white linen shirt. Women wear *Dirndl* – a dress with a full skirt that goes down to the knee (at least) and a close-fitting bodice, usually with criss-crossing laces to pull it tighter. Under the *Dirndl* women wear a blouse, with an apron over the outfit to complete the costume.

Since 2005 families and old aged pensioners have been encouraged to attend, and new rules were brought in to make them feel welcome. Until 6pm only quiet music is allowed, at a maximum of 85 decibels. There is a special tent, called the *Augustiner*, for families, with activities for children. Every Tuesday is Family Day when there is a friendly family atmosphere.

Teaching Activities

◆ Imagine you are in Munich, Germany for the Oktoberfest. What can you see and hear? Which food are you going to choose to eat? (See photocopiable resource page 73.)

◆ Draw and label some German food on offer at Oktoberfest (see Schlüsselwörter box and Das Essen, pages 29–34, for vocabulary).

◆ Draw and label a German man and woman in traditional Bavarian costume.

◆ Celebrate Oktoberfest in class. Wear clothes in the colour of the German flag and taste some German food. Celebrate outside if possible, with some Bavarian music playing in the background. Encourage the children to say *Bitte* and *Danke* and to ask for food in German.

◆ Listen to the German national anthem, *Das Deutschlandlied*, which can be found on the Internet. Examine the words in both German and English. You could compare to to the British national anthem.

Schlüsselwörter

das Bier	beer
der Steinkrug	traditional beer mug
Märzen	dark, strong beer brewed for Oktoberfest
die Weißwürste	white veal sausages eaten at Oktoberfest
der Bratwurst	traditional German pork and veal sausage
das Hendl	whole spit roast chicken
der Käse	cheese
das Sauerkraut	pickled cabbage
Dampfnudel	steamed yeast dumpling
der Kaiserschmarrn	sugared pancake with raisins
der Apfelpfannenkuchen	apple pancakes

Einigkeit und Recht und Freiheit	Unity and law and freedom
für das deutsche Vaterland!	For the German Fatherland!
Danach lasst uns alle streben	Let us all strive for that
Brüderlich mit Herz und Hand!	In brotherhood with heart and hand!
Einigkeit und Recht und Freiheit	Unity and law and freedom
Sind des Glückes Unterpfand;	Are the foundation for happiness;
Blüh' im Glanze dieses Glückes,	Bloom in the glow of happiness,
Blühe, deutsches Vaterland.	Bloom, German Fatherland.

This song has been the German national anthem since 1922, although at times the words have been changed or verses added or dropped. The music was written by Joseph Haydn in 1797 as an anthem for the birthday of the Austrian Emperor Francis II of the Holy Roman Empire and the original words were written in 1841 by the German linguist and poet, August Heinrich Hoffmann von Fallersleben. They were considered revolutionary at the time. Since reunification in 1991, only the third stanza (shown above) is used as the national anthem.

◆ Draw and colour the image that *Das Deutschlandlied* creates in your mind.

German Festivals and Traditions
© Nicolette Hannam, Michelle Williams and Brilliant Publications

Oktoberfest

Name: Datum:

I understand how and why Oktoberfest is celebrated in Germany.

Imagine you are standing among the tents at Oktoberfest. It is very busy with lots of laughter and music. Many people are eating and drinking.

What can you see?

What can you hear?

What will you choose to eat for your dinner today?

What are people wearing?

Extension activity

Draw and label a picture on the back of this sheet of your description. Include as much detail as you can.

Comparing buildings and places

Background information

Germany is densely populated with people living in large cities, towns and small villages. In towns and villages generations of families tend to settle and stay living near each other. German towns usually have a market place, a town hall, and a range of large and small shops. Main shopping areas are pedestrianized and, in the summer, cafés spread out onto the streets.

Teaching activities

◆ Children could use photocopiable page 75 to draw and label a German town. There is then the opportunity to compare it to the children's home town.

◆ Compare other buildings and places in a town. Children could draw their local town centre and label it in German.

◆ Children could use dictionaries to look up different buildings in their own town, for example, a library.

◆ Link to Maths. Children could use co-ordinates to direct each other around a German town to do their shopping. (See Schlüsselwörter box for vocabulary.)

◆ Children could design and make a board game based on places in a German town centre.

◆ Children could role play buying items in a shop, first as a whole class and then in small groups or pairs. They could extend their learning by adding size or colour information.

◆ Give children names of buildings to put in dictionary order.

◆ Can you plan some activities for German children to do in school to teach them about Britain? Who could they learn about? What music could they listen to? Which places should they find on a map? See guided sheet on page 76.

Schlüsselwörter

der Marktplatz	a market place
das Rathaus	a town hall
das Verkehrsamt	Tourist information centre
die Konditorei	cake shop
die Bäckerei	bakery
die Metzgerei	butcher's shop
die Apotheke	chemists
der Supermarkt	supermarket
die Sparkasse	bank
die Geschäfte	shops
geradeaus	straight on
halt	stop
Gehen Sie	go
Gehen Sie nach links	turn left
Gehen Sie nach rechts	turn right
Gehen Sie zurück	go back

Comparing buildings and places

Name: Datum:

I can compare buildings in a German town to the buildings in my home town.

Use the words below to draw and label a typical German town and its buildings. Start with the market place in the middle, and the town hall. Then add some shops and cafes.

der Marketplatz	a market place	die Konditorei	cake shop
das Rathaus	a town hall	die Bäckerei	bakery
das Verkehrsamt	Tourist Information Centre	die Metzgerei	butcher

---

Meine Stadt
My German town

Extension activity

Which buildings are the same in your home town? Which buildings are different?

What I know about Germany

Name: Datum:

I can think about what I already know and what I would like to find out about Germany.

What do you already know about Germany?

What would you like to find out?

How can you find out this information?

What could you tell a German person about your country and your culture?

Extension activity

What activities could German children do in school to help them learn about Britain?

German Festivals and Traditions
© Nicolette Hannam, Michelle Williams and Brilliant Publications

Martinstag
St Martin's Day

Background information

St Martin was a fourth Century Roman soldier from Tours, who later become a monk. Because of his exemplary way of life, he was later appointed Bishop of Tours (against his will). According to legend he did many good deeds, including cutting his cloak in half to share with a beggar who was dying in the cold.

St Martin's Day is celebrated on 11th November (the same day when many other countries celebrate Remembrance Day). People (mostly children) walk in processions called *St. Martins-Umzüge,* holding lanterns (usually self-made). At the front of the procession is a man riding a horse, dressed as St Martin. People sing a traditional St Martin's Day song which praises the saint's generosity. The procession often ends with a bonfire after which children often go from door to door singing songs. They are given candy, money and other goodies as a reward for their singing.

The day is also linked with the end of the harvest season and the start of winter. The symbol of St. Martin's day is the goose and some German people celebrate by eating roast goose. Legend has it that Martin was reluctant to be appointed as bishop so he hid in a goose pen. The squawking geese gave him away and because of this they are eaten on this day.

St Martin's Day is also the official start of Karneval, at 11 minutes past 11 on the 11th day of the 11th month. It's at this time that carnival clubs and neighbourhood groups start their preparations for the carnival season that culminates with the big Fasching (Mardi Gras) parades in February (see pages 15–18).

Teaching activities

◆ Make paper lanterns and hold your own St Martinstag parade.

◆ Which good deeds have you done this week? Can you plan one a day for the next week? What are they? Who will benefit from them?

◆ If you were made a Saint and had a day named after you, how would you like people to celebrate? What could they do and eat?

◆ Can you make up a song, in English, about St Martin using the facts you have learnt? You could use a familiar tune.

Schlüsselwörter

der Umzug	parade
die Laterne	lantern
singen	to sing
die Gans	goose

Challenging stereotypes

Background information

Everyone has visual images in their heads of places they have never been to and people they have never met. Even after visiting a country, a full picture may not have been acquired. Stereotypical expectations of German people are that they wear Lederhosen, drink beer and eat sausages! Perhaps a little exaggerated! Stereotypical images of British people are that they always carry umbrellas, drink tea and speak with posh accents. Stereotypes can be identified for many countries and cultures, and are often very inaccurate.

Stereotypes need to be addressed, discussed, challenged and corrected. It is a subject that can be discussed as part of many lessons, or even after playground fallouts. After discussion, children will conclude that German children are very similar to themselves, with some distinct cultural differences that should be explored and celebrated.

Teaching activities

◆ Class discussion: What is a stereotype? Can you think of any examples?

◆ Discuss children's visual images of a stereotypical German person, and ask them for their reasons/evidence. Use the photocopiable guided sheet on page 79 to compare stereotypical views of German and British people with more realistic views.

◆ Brainstorm other types of stereotypes that exist. Are they positive or negative? Discuss.

German Festivals and Traditions
© Nicolette Hannam, Michelle Williams and Brilliant Publications

Challenging stereotypes

Name: Datum:

I recognize that stereotypes are often inaccurate.

Look at the pictures below of stereotypical German and British people. In the boxes underneath draw a more realistic picture of each person, based on the knowledge you have gained in your language lessons.

A stereotypical German person	A stereotypical British person

A realistic German person	A realistic British person

Role models for children

Background information

All children need good role models. Although different in each culture, common themes will remain. Children should be encouraged to look up to authors, sports people and so on. This will help them to become ambitious. It can provide them with real-life reasons to perform and achieve well at school.

Examples of good role models in Britain are David Beckham and J K Rowling. In Germany, children admire Michael Schumacher and Claudia Schiffer.

Full name:	Claudia Schiffer
Date of birth:	25. August 1970
Place of birth:	Düsseldorf, Germany
Height:	1.82 m

Claudia Schiffer was just 17 when, at a disco, she was spotted by a representative for a modelling agency. Six months later, after graduating from high school, she made her first appearance on the cover of *Elle* magazine. Since then she has gone on to become a supermodel, appearing on over 700 magazine covers.

She has appeared in advertisements for a wide range of items - from jeans and other clothing to make-up, cars and champagne. Once she even danced with a cartoon version of Mickey Mouse in an advertisement to promote Fanta!

Claudia has also appeared in a number of films and music videos. She speaks English and French, as well as German.

Full name:	Michael Schumacher
Nicknames:	Schumi, Schuey
Date of birth:	3. January 1969
Place of birth	Hürth-Hermülheim, Germany
Height	1.74 m

Michael Schumacher is widely regarded as the world's best ever racing driver. In 1995 he became (at that time) the youngest person to win the Formula I World Championship two times in a row. He went on to win the Championship 7 times, beating the previous world record.

He also holds the Formula I records for most career wins, most wins in a season, most points during a season, most podium finishes, most fastest laps and many others!

Since the end of 2006 he has worked as a consultant to the car firm, Ferrari. He advises them on race and road car development and helps support their current Formula 1 drivers.

Teaching activities

◆ Talk about what makes a good role model.

◆ Children could discuss their role models. Who? Why?

◆ Children could draw a picture of their role model and write reasons around it.

◆ Children could draw and research a German role model.

◆ Children could compare a German role model to a British one.

◆ Children could write an acrostic poem using 'Role Model' or the name of their chosen role model.

Weihnachten
Christmas

Background information

Christmas is an important time of the year in Germany. Most people have an advent wreath (with four candles), and light one candle on each Sunday leading to Christmas Day. Christmas markets (*Weihnachtsmärkte*) are extremely popular, and most towns have one. They have many stalls that sell wooden toys, Christmas decorations, sweets, food and drink. At the centre of the market there is a nativity scene using wooden figures. Sometimes they have real people playing Maria and Josef, and even real animals. One of the most famous markets is in Nuremburg.

6th December, St Nikolaus

On the night before, children put their shoes outside their bedroom door for St Nikolaus. If they have been good they will be filled with presents, often sweets, in the morning. Traditionally, naughty children receive a piece of coal (but this tradition has largely been forgotten). According to legend, St Nikolaus was a bishop. He is usually pictured dressed in a white coat, with a white bishop's hat (a mitre) and a bishop's rod. He carries a golden book that says if a child was naughty or nice during the last year. With him is his helper, a dark scary figure, dressed in black, called 'Knecht Rupprecht', 'Krampus' or 'Schmutzli', depending on the region. 'Knecht Rupprecht' carries a birch stick to deter children from being bad in the coming year. Sometimes at Christmas parties, St Nikolaus will visit (one can hire them). He'll tell funny stories, often in rhyme about the people at the party, mentioning funny or even embarrassing events that happened during the last year.

24th December, Heiligabend (Holy Evening)

This is the most important day of the festive season in Germany. Traditionally German people put their tree up on Christmas Eve, using a lot of dark green and red for their decorations. Many people go to church and attend Midnight Mass. Often, during the service, some children may act out the Christmas story. After church families sit down to a big meal and open their presents. Traditionally presents were brought by the *Christkind* (baby Jesus), and in some families that is still the case. In others, the presents are brought by Father Christmas, known as *Weihnachtsmann*. The *Christkind* is pictured as a pretty child with blond curly hair, dressed in a white and golden dress. He is accompanied by little angels, who prepare the toys and presents for the children (instead of the elves who help Father Christmas).

25th December, Erster Weihnachtstag

Christmas day is a public holiday in Germany. People usually have dinner with their relatives. A traditional Christmas dinner includes roast goose (see also Christmas food on page 82).

26ᵗʰ December, Zweiter Weihnachtstag

The day after Christmas is also a public holiday. People continue to spend time with family and friends and enjoy lots of food and drink. In some parts of Germany it is tradition to visit friends to praise their tree. This is called 'Christbaumloben' and people say 'Ein schöner Baum!' (What a nice tree!). They then sit down for a drink together.

Christmas food

There are many type of food associated with Christmas time:

Das Christbaumgebäck	Christmas tree pastry, used to make the decorations for the Christmas tree.
Der Christstollen	Bread with nuts, raisins, lemon and dried fruit, and icing sugar on the top.
Der Lebkuchen	Ginger spice biscuits (see recipe on page 86).

A typical Christmas dinner is *Weihnachtsgans mit Kastanien und Backpflaumen* (Christmas goose with chestnuts and prunes) which they would eat with potatoes and vegetables. Dessert is usually *der Christstollen*.

31ˢᵗ December, Silvester

German people celebrate New Year's Eve with big parties, dancing and games. An old Silvester custom is called Bleigießen. It involves heating up a small amount of lead on a spoon over a small flame. You then pour the liquid lead into a bowl of cold water. The shape that is created can be used to predict your future for the year ahead. Here are some interpretations:

English	German	Meaning
ball	der Ball	Luck will roll your way
flower	die Blume	New friendship
fish	der Fisch	Luck
triangle	das Dreieck	Financial improvement
heart	das Herz	Fall in love
(eye)glasses	die Brille	Wisdom

At midnight people toast each other with sparkling wine or champagne and wish each other 'Ein schönes neues jahr!'. Then many fireworks are set off in celebration.

A strange New Year's Eve Custom

On New Year's Eve in Germany, it has become traditional to watch on TV a short British cabaret sketch set in the 1920s called, 'Dinner for One' or 'The 90ᵗʰ Birthday.' It is strange to think that it is unknown in Britain, even though this is where it was created! The film lasts about 20 minutes, and you could spend all evening watching it, because all the channels will show it at least once on New Year's Eve!

Teaching activities

◆ Compare British and German Christmas celebrations. using the Venn diagram on photocopiable page 88.

◆ Write to a real or imaginary German pen pal explaining what you eat for Christmas Dinner.

◆ Use a dictionary to translate the foods we eat at Christmas.

◆ Children could taste German Christstollen and wish each other *Fröhliche Weihnachten*.

◆ Children could write a letter to *Weihnachtsmann* using the photocopiable frame on page 87.

Vocabulary for the letter	
Lieber Weihnachtsmann	Dear Father Christmas
Ich möchte gerne …	I would like…
bitte	please
vielen dank	thank you very much

◆ Children could make nativity characters and put them together as a class tableau, or draw and label a nativity scene in German.

die Kuh — der Esel — Das Christkind/Jesus — die Krippe — Maria — Josef — der Schäfer — das Schaf — das Pferd

◆ Children could dress up as nativity characters and try a brief role play in German using simple greetings and questions.

◆ Draw and label a Christmas tree (ein Weihnachtsbaum). Add decorations and describe colours.

◆ Children could draw and label some presents they would like to receive. They could also draw and label some presents they would like to give to family members.

◆ Make *Lebkuchen* using the recipes on page 86.

◆ Children could mime making the *Lebkuchen* as you describe the actions in German (see recipe on page 86).

◆ Design and make a recipe card for the *Lebkuchen* recipe.

◆ Hold a 'Design a *Lebkuchen'* competition – draw and design your own ginger biscuit!

◆ Children could draw and label a traditional German Christmas dinner.

◆ Listen to some traditional Christmas carols, in both languages, and compare. Use page 85 as support. The music for *Stille Nacht* (Slient Night) is available on The Internet.

◆ Children could copy a short carol out in their best handwriting and decorate it for display.

◆ Make German Christmas cards.

German Festivals and Traditions
© *Nicolette Hannam, Michelle Williams and Brilliant Publications*

Christmas carol

Stille Nacht

Stille Nacht! Heilige Nacht!
Alles schläft' einsam wacht
nur das traute hochheilige Paar.
Holder Knabe im lockigen Haar,
schlaf in himmlischer Ruh,
schlaf in himmlischer Ruh.

Stille Nacht! Heilige Nacht!
Gottes Sohn, o wie lacht
Lieb' aus deinem göttlichen Mund,
Da uns schlägt die rettende Stund'.
Christ, in deiner Geburt!
Christ, in deiner Geburt!

Lebkuchen (ginger spice biscuits)

Traditionally eaten at Christmas.

Ingredients
1 kg flour
500g honey
250g sugar
50g butter
4 eggs
200g almonds (*finely chopped*)
50g diced lemon
50g diced orange
½ teaspoon ginger
½ teaspoon cloves
½ teaspoon cinnamon

Ingredients for sugar glaze
1 cup icing sugar
1 egg white
1–2 teaspoons lemon juice
Mix together to make the glaze.

Instructions
◆ Melt the honey and sugar together.

◆ Add the spices and let the mixture cool.

◆ Mix all the ingredients together. Make a smooth dough and leave for 24 hours.

◆ Roll out to 5mm thick. Use cutters to create different shapes.

◆ Bake in the oven for 12–15 minutes at 180°C/350°F.

◆ Decorate with the sugar glaze.

Zutaten
1 kg Mehl
500g Honig
250g Zucker
50g Butter
5 Eier
200g Mandel (*gerieben*)
50g Zitrone (*gehackt*)
50g Apfelsine (*gehackt*)
½ Teelöffel Ingwer
½ Teelöffel Gewürznelke
½ Teelöffel Zimt

Zuckerguß Zutaten
1 Tasse Puderzucker
1 Eiweiß
1–2 Teelöffel Zitronensaft
Die Zutaten gut verrühren.

Zubereitung
◆ Honig und Zucker in einem Topf erhitzen.

◆ Die Gewürze in den Topf geben und abkühlen lassen.

◆ Alle Zutaten miteinander vermengen, zu einem Teig verkneten und über Nacht bei Raumtemperatur ruhen lassen.

◆ Den Lebkuchen 5mm dick ausrollen und beliebige Formen ausstechen.

◆ Bei 180°C /350°F 10 bis 12–15 Minuten hellbraun backen.

◆ Mit Zuckerguß verzieren.

German Festivals and Traditions
© Nicolette Hannam, Michelle Williams and Brilliant Publications

Weihnachten

Name: Datum:

I can write a short letter to *der Weihnachtsmann*.

Weihnachten

Name: Datum:

I can compare Christmas and New Year traditions in the United Kingdom and Germany.

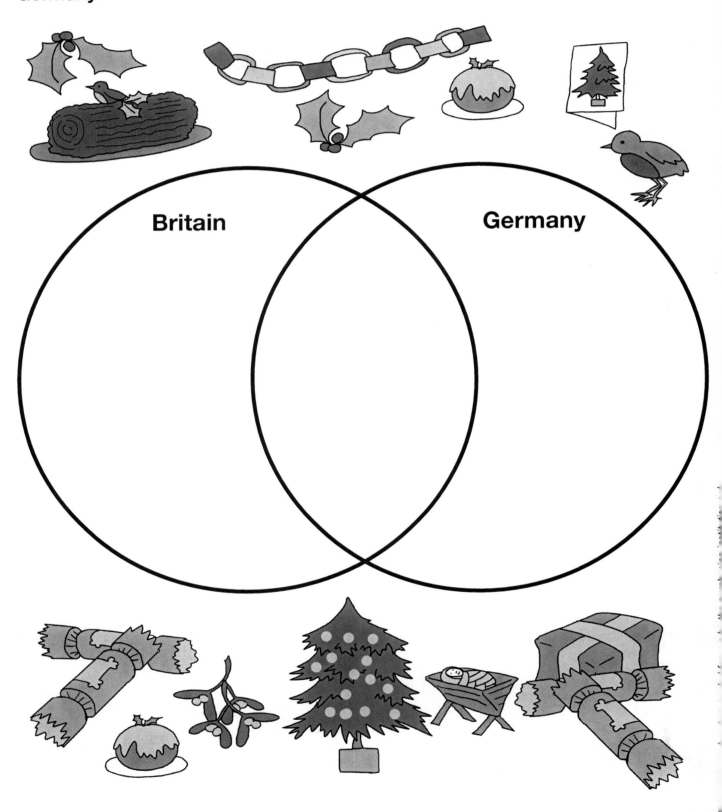

Britain   Germany

German Festivals and Traditions
© Nicolette Hannam, Michelle Williams and Brilliant Publications

Planning a German Day for your school

A German Day can help to raise the profile of Modern Foreign Languages and give staff and children the chance to enjoy the language as a large group. You can celebrate previous successes and enthuse pupils about future learning. To give the day a bigger impact, staff and children can be asked to wear black, red and yellow – the colours of the German flag.

When organizing the day, we recommend you provide teachers with all the resources they will need, to help alleviate stress and to allow them to participate fully in the day and enjoy themselves. On the following pages you will find lesson plans and photocopiable resources for the following four tried and tested activities:

Activity A – Gerhard Richter
Learning about the German artist, Gerhard Richter, and working as a class to produce an enlarged copy of one of his paintings.

Activity B – German food
Food tasting and making a place mat.

Activity C – Parachute activities and learning a song
Parachute activities following German instructions.
Learn a song and some actions for everyone to perform together in the final assembly.

Activity D – Classroom activity
Playing board games using German language.

We recommend having two assemblies: one in the morning to explain what will happen and set the tone for the day, and one at the end, so that you can celebrate your achievements. Here is a possible timetable:

Class	Session 1		Session 2		Session 3	Session 4	
1	Classroom activity	Registration	Parachute, then song	Playtime	Art	Food tasting	Assembly – sing the song learned during day and share work/ideas
2	Classroom activity		Song, then parachute		Food tasting	Art	
3	Art		Food tasting		Parachute, then song	Classroom activity	
4	Food tasting		Art		Song, then parachute	Classroom activity	
5	Art		Food tasting		Classroom activity	Parachute, then song	
6	Food tasting		Art		Classroom activity	Song, then parachute	
7	Parachute, then song		Classroom activity		Food tasting	Art	
8	Song, then parachute		Classroom activity		Art	Food tasting	

(Between Session 1 and Session 2: Assembly – sing some songs children have already learned. Explanation of day's activities. Between Session 2 and Session 3: Dinnertime.)

The pupil evaluation sheet on pages 98–99 can be used to reinforce intercultural understanding and will help you to develop ideas further.

Activity A - Gerhard Richter

Objectives
◆ To learn about Gerhard Richter.
◆ To make a class painting.

Background information
◆ He was born on February 9th, 1932 in Dresden, Germany.
◆ He first became noticed when he painted a giant mural on the wall as his final piece of work at college.
◆ He taught Art in his early career.
◆ He now lives in Düsseldorf.
◆ He has been married three times and has one son and two daughters.
◆ He had his first solo exhibition in 1964.
◆ His paintings are very varied, including many abstract landscapes.
◆ Some of his paintings have sold for a million dollars.
◆ He is known by some as the greatest living painter.

Resources provided by MFL Coordinator
• A4 colour copies of Richter paintings from the Internet, cut into 15 and numbered on the back. (You will need to do enough for each pupil to have one small piece of the painting)
• Examples of Gerhard Richter's paintings for display on whiteboard

Class teacher will need to provide
• A4 cartridge paper (for children to paint on)
• Selection of paints and painting equipment

Teaching activities
◆ Talk to the class about Gerhard Richter and show copies of some of his paintings.

◆ Give children one piece each of the Gerhard Richter painting and ask them to paint a copy of their small section onto an A4 sheet. They will need to take care enlarging it, and think carefully about their colour mixing.

◆ At the end of the session each painting can be pieced together, using the numbers on the back of the original pieces the children were given, like a big jigsaw. The end result is a large copy of Gerhard Richter's painting and a ready made display.

◆ You could talk about the colours of the painting in German, and children could be encouraged to form an opinion of the class masterpiece, again in German. The following vocabulary will help:

Es ist super/toll	It's great.
Ich mag es!	I like it!
Ich mag es nicht!	I don't like it!
Die Farben	**Colours**
Rot	red
Blau	blue
Grün	green
Gelb	yellow
Schwarz	black
Weiß	white
Orange	orange

Activity B – German food

Objectives

◆ To taste some German food.
◆ To know how to ask for the food in German.
◆ To know the German names of some fruit and vegetables.
◆ To make a place mat.

Teaching activities

◆ Prepare some German food for the children to taste. Encourage them to ask for it in German (see below).

◆ Before tasting the food teach the names of fruit and vegetables in German.

◆ Explain the phrases 'Ich mag' for 'I like' and 'Ich mag nicht' for 'I don't like' so that children can complete them on their place mats. Also teach the following:

Ich möchte …	I would like …
Bitte	Please
Danke	Thank you

◆ Then provide each child with a place mat frame to decorate during the lesson, together with laminated copies of the sheets of fruits and vegetables (one per table). The place mats can later be laminated and sent home.

◆ Whilst the children work, take around the food for them to try. Play some German music, if you have a CD, to help to pretend that you really are in Germany!

◆ What could children ask for and how?

Ich möchte das Brot, bitte.	I would like some bread, please.
Ich möchte der Käse, bitte.	I would like some cheese, please.
Ich möchte die Wurst, bitte.	I would like some sausage, please.
Ich möchte Lebkuchen, bitte.	I would like some Lebkuchen, please.
Ich möchte den Orangensaft, bitte.	I would like some orange juice, please.
Ich möchte heiße Schokolade, bitte.	I would like a hot chocolate, please.

◆ Encourage them to say *Vielen Dank* (thank you very much!)

Resources provided by MFL Coordinator

• German food and drink (eg bread, cheese, sausages, Lebkuchen, orange juice and hot chocolate)
• Cups, plates
• Laminated sheets of fruit and vegetables and their names in German, one per table (pages 92–93)
• Place mat frames (page 94)
• German music
• CD and CD player
• Laminating pouches for completed place mats

Class teacher will need to provide

• Colouring pencils
• Pencils/pens

Obst

der Apfel

die Birne

die Erdbeeren

die Melone

die Kirschen

die Pfirsich

die Pampelmuse

die Banane

die Ananas

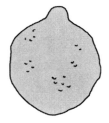

die Zitrone

die Orange

die Trauben

German Festivals and Traditions
© *Nicolette Hannam, Michelle Williams and Brilliant Publications*

Gemüse

die Zwiebel

die Kartoffel

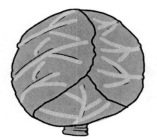

der Kohl

der Champignon

die Erbsen

die Karotte

die Gurke

der Paprika

die Brokkoli

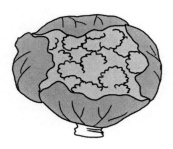

der Blumenkohl

die Aubergine

der Mais

Ich mag nicht

Ich mag

Activity C – Parachute games and a song to learn

Objectives

◆ To participate in some German-themed parachute games.
◆ To learn a song and some actions to sing with everyone in the assembly at the end of the day.

Resources provided by MFL Coordinator

• Parachute
• A laminated copy of this sheet
• CD and song sheet for chosen song – there are many German song books with CDs to choose from.
• CD player

Teaching activities

◆ There are two activities to complete this session. Each class needs time in the hall or the playground to try some parachute games. Start with teaching the children simple instructions in German:

Links	Left
Rechts	Right
Gehen	Walk
Halt	Stop
Schneller	Faster
Langsamer	Slower
Höher	Higher
Niedriger	Lower

◆ Then teach the following games. Call out instructions in German.

Die Nummern (numbers)

Give each child a number from 1–5: eins, zwei, drei, vier, fünf. When you call out a number, those children run round to a new place.

Katze und Maus (cat and mouse)

Everyone holds the parachute stretched out at about waist height. Someone becomes a mouse and goes underneath. Someone else becomes a cat and goes on top. The rest of the group try to hide the mouse by moving the chute up and down.

Champignon (mushroom)

Can you all stretch the parachute above your heads, pull it down behind you and sit down with it under your bottom to form a mushroom shape? Once inside your mushroom you could count around the circle in German, name colours, etc.

◆ Back in class pupils can listen to a song and learn the words. It is even more fun if everyone learns the same actions as well. The song can be performed as a very large group in assembly.

Activity D – Classroom activity

Objective
◆ To use German vocabulary when playing co-operatively.

Teaching activities
◆ This activity consists of a selection of games the children can choose to play in pairs or small groups.

◆ Give each pair or group a laminated card of vocabulary to help them speak some German.

Resources provided by MFL Coordinator
• Suggested games: Snakes and Ladders, Ludo, Snap or Dominoes. There are many resources available as images on the Internet that can be colour printed and laminated (for example, Snakes and Ladders boards)
• Laminated cards to support vocabulary (page 97)

Class teacher will need to provide
• Colouring pencils
• Scissors
• Dice
• Counters

How to play games in German

◆ Choose a game to play with a friend or in a small group.

◆ Try to use some German language. Here are some useful phrases:

Would you like to play?	Möchtest du spielen?
Your turn.	Du bist dran.
My turn.	Ich bin dran.
You win.	Du hast gewonnen.
I win.	Ich habe gewonnen.

◆ Say the number on the dice aloud.

◆ Count in German as you move along the board:

eins	one
zwei	two
drei	three
vier	four
fünf	five
sechs	six
sieben	seven
acht	eight
neun	nine
zehn	ten
elf	eleven
zwölf	twelve

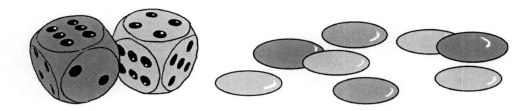

Ein deutscher Tag

Name: Datum:

I have participated in our German Day.

Draw and describe the activities that took place in the box below.

Which activities did you enjoy? Explain why.

What did you learn?

Ask a friend what they enjoyed most and why.

Which activities would you plan for German children whose school was having an English day?

Useful resources

Websites
Linguascope

Atantot

Resource books published by Brilliant Publications
Das ist Deutsch

Wir Spielen Zusammen

German Pen Pals Made Easy

Deutsch-Lotto

Gute Idee

Lightning Source UK Ltd.
Milton Keynes UK
04 January 2010

148150UK00001B/2/P